THE SUPERHERO ULTRAFERNO

A full-length comedy by
Don Zolidis

www.youthplays.com
info@youthplays.com
424-703-5315

COPYRIGHT RULES TO REMEMBER

1. To produce this play, you must receive prior written permission from YouthPLAYS and pay the required royalty.

2. You must pay a royalty each time the play is performed in the presence of audience members outside of the cast and crew. Royalties are due whether or not admission is charged, whether or not the play is presented for profit, for charity or for educational purposes, or whether or not anyone associated with the production is being paid.

3. No changes, including cuts or additions, are permitted to the script without written prior permission from YouthPLAYS.

4. Do not copy this book or any part of it without written permission from YouthPLAYS.

5. Credit to the author and YouthPLAYS is required on all programs and other promotional items associated with this play's performance.

When you pay royalties, you are recognizing the hard work that went into creating the play and making a statement that a play is something of value. We think this is important, and we hope that everyone will do the right thing, thus allowing playwrights to generate income and continue to create wonderful new works for the stage.

Plays are owned by the playwrights who wrote them. Violating a playwright's copyright is a very serious matter and violates both United States and international copyright law. Infringement is punishable by actual damages and attorneys' fees, statutory damages of up to $150,000 per incident, and even possible criminal sanctions. **Infringement is theft. Don't do it.**

Have a question about copyright? Please contact us by email at info@youthplays.com or by phone at 424-703-5315. When in doubt, please ask.

CAST OF CHARACTERS

NARRATOR 1 (female)	JOLENE
NARRATOR 2 (male)	BOY
SPENCER	GIRL
MELVIN	BOY 2
BURT	GIRL 2

Part 1: Batman

BATMAN	CLARK (SUPERMAN)
ROBIN	

Part 2: Wonder Woman

WONDER WOMAN	AMAZONIAN QUEEN
BLACK CANARY	BOSS 1-4
WHITE QUEEN	SECRETARY
HULK	

Part 3: Superman

AQUAMAN	INS AGENT 1
JOR-EL	INS AGENT 2
LARAMOM	MAN 1
DAD	MAN 2

Part 4: The Avengers

HAWKEYE	THOR
NATASHA	SALESGIRL
STEVE	GIRL 3
BRUCE	JENNIFER
TONY	

Part 5: The X-Men

MOM 2

DAD 2

ANGELICA

PROFESSOR XAVIER

WOLVERINE

STUDENT

Part 6: Wolverine

DISNEY EXEC 1

DISNEY EXEC 2

WOLVIE

MOTHER

MONGO

BRUTUS

PRINCE

Part 7: Dr. and Mrs. Doom

DR. DOOM

MRS. DOOM

Part 8: The Fantastic Four

SCOTT

NURSE

NURSE 2

REED

SUE

JOHNNY

JILL

WRITER 1

WRITER 2

GALACTUS

Part 9: Doctor Strange

EXECUTIVE 1

EXECUTIVE 2

DOCTOR STRANGE

DOCTOR DRUID

SCARLET WITCH

ANNOUNCER

MODRED THE MYSTIC

CARLY

Part 10: Batman vs. Superman

Part 11: Spiderman

PETER PARKER

STUDENTS

<table>
<tr><td>MARY JANE WATSON</td><td>AUNT MAY</td></tr>
<tr><td>MAD SCIENTIST</td><td>GREEN GOBLIN</td></tr>
<tr><td>POLICE OFFICER 1</td><td>DOCTOR OCTOPUS</td></tr>
<tr><td>POLICE OFFICER 2</td><td>BLACK CAT</td></tr>
<tr><td>ANNOUNCER</td><td>ELECTRO</td></tr>
<tr><td>ROBBER</td><td>SANDMAN</td></tr>
<tr><td>UNCLE BEN</td><td></td></tr>
</table>

NOTES

How to Perform this Play: This is a very fast-moving show with lots of roles. The best way to do it is to show the wires, so to speak. Allow the costume changes to be very minor – for the heroes, perhaps using only a mask, or a cape, or something to signify their character, is best. Speed is really important to something like this, so don't get bogged down with set changes either. If pieces can be moved on and off with lightning speed, then go for it, but otherwise there is very little scenery needed.

Gender of Characters: Most superheroes are male. I make a lot of jokes about this. I have no problem with performers of any gender playing any of the male roles. They should be played as men, though. I don't think it works as well with "Batgirl" instead of "Batman," for instance. The parts for women (Wonder Woman, Amazonian Queen, Scarlet Witch, etc.), should stay women.

I've written almost all of the other roles as gender neutral (Writer, Disney Exec, Students…) and these can be any gender, too.

Ethnicity of Characters: Same thing for ethnicity. I do make jokes about Superman and Aquaman being white, but there's no reason an actor of color couldn't play those roles. All of the heroes are archetypes, and have been played by different actors over the years. So please feel free to have any actor of any race or ethnicity in any part.

Ad-Libbing: This kind of play works fine with ad-libbing, particularly by the Narrators who are guiding the action. If you come up with something particularly brilliant, go ahead and use it in the show.

Cutting: For time, or for community standards, you may cut any section of the play as necessary. You could easily do only eight sections of the play, for instance. The act break is optional, so you may do the show with or without a break.

One Last Thing: Resist the urge to mug to the audience. Unless it's part of their character, all of the superheroes should be deadly serious. It's funnier if they don't know they're funny.

Also: This is parody, so I hope DC or Marvel doesn't sue me. I'm a big fan.

ACKNOWLEDGEMENTS

The Superhero Ultraferno (full-length) had its world premiere at The Gregory School in Tucson, Arizona, on October 22-23, 2015. It was directed by Lisa Bodden and the original cast was as follows:

NARRATOR 1	Alexandra Nesci
NARRATOR 2	Daniel Rosenberg
SPENCER	Spencer Martin
MELVIN	Oliver Bates

BURT	Brian Evans
JOLENE	Devin Johnston
BOY	Brian Liu
GIRL	Yuyao Hu
BOY 2	Guanhong Chen
GIRL 2	Téa Weiner

Part 1: Batman

BATMAN	Brian Evans
ROBIN	Nina Armstrong
CLARK	Kai Morfin

Part 2: Wonder Woman

WOMAN	Lourdes Castillo Silva
BLACK CANARY	Yuxi Xia
QUEEN	Lauren Westphal
HULK	Brian Liu
AMAZONIAN QUEEN	Chloé Goorman
BOSS 1	Kai Morfin
BOSS 2	Oliver Bates
BOSS 3	Brian Evans
BOSS 4	Spencer Martin
SECRETARY	Téa Weiner

Part 3: Superman

AQUAMAN	Oliver Bates
JOR-EL	Lauren Westphal
LARA	Sedona Naifeh
MOM	Yuxi Xia
DAD	Guanhong Chen
INS AGENT 1	Lily Cate Smith
INS AGENT 2	Lauren Westphal
MAN 1	Devin Johnston
MAN 2	Brian Evans

Part 4: The Avengers
HAWKEYE   Kai Morfin
NATASHA   Caroline Zlaket
STEVE   Tanaya Davis
BRUCE   Brian Liu
TONY   Spencer Martin
THOR   Sedona Naifeh
SALESGIRL   Chloé Goorman
GIRL 3   Lily Cate Smith
JENNIFER   Lauren Westphal

Part 5: The X-Men
MOM 2   Yuxi Xia
ANGELICA   Devin Johnston
PROFESSOR XAVIER   Lourdes Castillo Silva
WOLVERINE   Yuyao Hu
STUDENT   Téa Weiner

Part 6: Wolverine
DISNEY EXECUTIVE 1   Lily Cate Smith
DISNEY EXECUTIVE 2   Sedona Naifeh
WOLVIE   Lauren Westphal
MOTHER   Yuxi Xia
MONG   Tanaya Davis
BRUTUS   Kai Morfin
PRINCE   Brian Evans

Part 7: Dr. and Mrs. Doom
DR. DOOM   Spencer Martin
MRS. DOOM   Lourdes Castillo Silva

Part 8: The Fantastic Four
SCOTT   Sedona Naifeh
NURSE   Chloé Goorman
NURSE 2   Daniel Rosenberg
REED   Oliver Bates

SUE   Alexandra Nesci
JOHNNY   Brian Evans
JILL   Téa Weiner
WRITER 1   Nina Armstrong
WRITER 2   Sedona Naifeh
GALACTUS   Yuxi Xia

Part 9: Doctor Strange
EXECUTIVE 1   Caroline Zlaket
EXECUTIVE 2   Lauren Westphal
DOCTOR STRANGE   Brian Liu
DOCTOR DRUID   Spencer Martin
SCARLET WITCH   Téa Weiner
ANNOUNCER   Chloé Goorman
MODRED THE MYSTIC   Lourdes Castillo Silva
CARLY   Sarah Mark

Part 10: Batman vs. Superman

Part 11: Spiderman
PETER PARKER   Daniel Rosenberg
STUDENTS   Tanaya Davis, Chloé
                             Goorman, Kai Morfin, Lily
                             Cate Smith, Téa Weiner,
                             Caroline Zlaket

MARY JANE WATSON   Lourdes Castillo Silva
MAD SCIENTIST   Tanaya Davis
FAME   Caroline Zlaket
MONEY   Kai Morfin
LADIES   Sedona Naifeh
POLICE 1   Nina Armstrong
POLICE 2   Devin Johnston
ANNOUNCER   Chloé Goorman
CRUSHER   Sedona Naifeh
ROBBER   Brian Liu

UNCLE BEN	Spencer Martin
AUNT MAY	Yuxi Xia
GREEN GOBLIN	Sedona Naifeh
DR. OCTOPUS	Chloé Goorman
BLACK CAT	Lily Cate Smith
ELECTRO	Brian Evans
SANDMAN	Lauren Westphal
SPIDER	Sarah Mark

Stage Manager, David Castillo; Assistant Stage Manager, Skylar Decker; House Manager, Sarah Mark; Costume Master, Nicholas McCullough; Hair and Makeup Manager, Ruby Meyer; Costume Crew, Ian Aaronson and Sarah Mark; Lighting Design, Ben Manninen; Sound Design, Dimitri Fleming, Israel Krzyz, and Yoni Weiner; Set Crew, Dennett Brown, Graham Gordon, James Kukla, Jacob Rosquist, Nick Rosquist; Properties Head, Kavi Koshkarian; Publicity Head, Ben Showard-Guerreo; Publicity Crew, Guanhong Chen, Dora Pezić, Victoria Sublett; Makeup Team, Ariana Deitch, Jessica Moore, Chloe Gardner; Hair Team, Elaine Wright.

ACT I

(The set can be very flexible. A typical American high school works for most settings. You could also do something abstract or stylized, like giant comic book covers.)

(Creepy music.)

(Perhaps fog.)

NARRATOR 1: Long, long ago in a galaxy far, far away...this sad scene was playing out in high schools all across the world.

(Lights on four stereotypical 80s-style nerds, SPENCER, MELVIN, BURT, and JOLENE.)

SPENCER: I'm tired of being picked on!

MELVIN: I just said that *Star Trek* was inherently superior to *Star Wars*, I wasn't picking on you.

SPENCER: Take that back! You take that back! Does *Star Trek* have Wookies?! No! It does not!

BURT: Oh please. *Star Wars* has magic. It's completely unrealistic.

SPENCER: The Force is not magic!

BURT: It's magic!

SPENCER: It is a fiber that binds the universe together with both a dark and a light side! I think I understand the Force, thank you very much.

JOLENE: All right Gandalf.

MELVIN: Jolene, how many times do I have to say it? No one cares about *Lord of the Rings* here.

JOLENE: Heathens!

SPENCER: Hey! Hey! Enough! Would the order of the Secret Anime, Robot, Superhero, and Fantasy Club please come to order?

MELVIN: Live long and prosper.

BURT: May the Force be with you.

JOLENE: Precious.

SPENCER: I have something to propose today to you. Something so radical it will reshape the very fabric of the planet. No more will we be relegated to the shadows watching the jocks get all the girls. No longer will we be teased, humiliated, forced into the toilet stalls —

JOLENE: You were forced into a toilet stall?

SPENCER: My grandmother is very strong. She's also vicious. Someday I will have my revenge.

BURT: So what were you saying?

SPENCER: Oh! Right. Gentlemen — and girl...I give you...THE PLAN.

(He hands out folders.)

JOLENE: Ooh I like the colored tabs.

BURT: Did you do these at Kinko's?

SPENCER: Yes I did and thank you for asking. Let's open them synchronously.

JOLENE: Ooh.

(They open them synchronously.)

MELVIN: Ha ha ha ha.

MELVIN AND BURT: Ha ha ha ha ha.

ALL FOUR: Moo aha ha ha ha ha.

NARRATOR 1: What was in that plan?

SPENCER: Can I explain it in an evil villain monologue?

NARRATOR 1: Go ahead.

SPENCER: Excellent. By now my plan is becoming increasingly clear.

JOLENE: Actually you spelled it out for us right here.

SPENCER: No I mean—just imagine I'm talking to a superhero who has come to confront us.

MELVIN: Ooh can I play the superhero?

SPENCER: Can I do my monologue please?

By now my plan is becoming increasingly clear. And there's nothing you can do to stop it. I'm afraid this battle station will be fully operational by the time your friends arrive. Even now my agents are infiltrating the major movie studios and television stations. You won't notice at first. Maybe a movie here, maybe an adaptation of Batman there. But rest assured, my masked friend, that is the only beginning. As my legion of geeks moves their way into positions of power, soon every movie will be a superhero movie. Every summer you and your friends will crowd into movie theatres to watch the things I loved as a kid. You won't be able to escape. We will run the show. AND THE GEEKS SHALL RULE THE WORLD! You think we'll stop with America? Oh no. Ha ha ha. We'll export the movies to China, and Europe, and Latin America even though that's still a relatively small market—everyone, everywhere in the world will worship our spandex-clad heroes! And we will be rich, I tell you! Rich! So rich that we will steal all your wives. Actually, scratch that. We will find younger, hotter women than your wives and we'll marry them and make you jealous!

JOLENE: Can we put something like and also male models in there?

SPENCER: Don't ruin this, Jolene! And then I've added Ha ha ha ha! Hooo ahh ha ha ha! Ha! Activate the tractor beam.

MOM: *(Off:)* Honey, what are you doing down there?

SPENCER: I'm busy, Mom!

MOM: *(Off:)* Do you guys want trail mix?

SPENCER: Yes! And leave it at the door!

MOM: *(Off:)* Would you also like Mountain Dew?

SPENCER: Of course we want Mountain Dew!

NARRATOR 1: And Spencer's plan succeeded beyond his wildest dreams. Soon they conquered Hollywood and made Comic Con the biggest event of the year. And the geeks walked upon the earth like giant dinosaurs snapping up popular kids and eating them in their gigantic jaws. Which is why we're here today.

(NARRATOR 2 enters.)

NARRATOR 2: THAT'S RIGHT! IT'S TIME FOR THE SUPERHERO ULTRAFERNO!

NARRATOR 1: Indeed it is.

NARRATOR 2: ULTRAFERNO!

NARRATOR 1: Not even a word.

NARRATOR 2: Where I'm coming from, we don't need words. Boom! *Back to the Future* reference. Who's with me?

NARRATOR 1: You'll have to excuse [Narrator 2's real name], he was raised by monkeys.

NARRATOR 2: Now we've heard that some of you might not have spent every waking hour reading comic books in your bedrooms.

NARRATOR 1: Losers.

NARRATOR 2: And you might need a primer on superheroes in order to participate in modern life. NOW THAT THE GEEKS RULE THE WORLD! High five! Who's with me? Any dorky people in the audience?

(He turns to Narrator 1.)

NARRATOR 1: I suppose.

NARRATOR 2: Yes! *(High five.)* You want to hug it out?

NARRATOR 1: No I do not.

NARRATOR 2: All right then.

NARRATOR 1: Let's take just a second to examine what has happened in modern high schools. This scenario, for instance, is all too common these days.

(BOY and GIRL enter, mid-conversation. He looks very dorky. She's beautiful.)

BOY: And he was telling me—I'm not a Shi'ar, I'm a Skrull.

GIRL: Ha ha ha ha! You are so funny!

BOY: That was actually a tragic statement. You see Skrulls have shape-shifting abilities whereas Shi'ar are descended from birds.

GIRL: Oh. Right. Yes I knew that.

BOY: I'm afraid I can't date you anymore. I must leave you now.

(GIRL 2 runs in.)

GIRL 2: Ooh! Go out with me instead!

BOY: I suppose. Come, I've equipped my car to look like Penguin's submarine.

GIRL 2: Yayyy!

(They exit, hand-in-hand.)

(Girl cries.)

GIRL: Nooo! I had my chance to hold on to him and I failed! If only I understood the properties of alien races! Why did I spend so much time not learning that?!

(She breaks down and cries as BOY 2, a jock, enters.)

BOY 2: Hey I'm the starting quarterback on the football team—

GIRL: Leave me alone, loser!

(Boy 2 runs off, crying.)

BOY 2: *(While running off:)* It hurts so much!

NARRATOR 1: Have no fear. We're here for you.

NARRATOR 2: We can teach you.

GIRL: But there's so much to know. And I'm just a girl.

NARRATOR 1: Wait, hold on—

GIRL: I can't possibly know about these things! My brain is already full of girl stuff like clothes and popular music!

NARRATOR 1: You know, this is kind of sexist here—

NARRATOR 2: Oh just wait, cause it's about to get way worse! High five!

NARRATOR 1: No. There are plenty of guys who don't know anything about comics either.

(Boy 2 returns.)

BOY 2: I've spent a lot of time in the gym building these awesome muscles.

NARRATOR 1: They look nice though.

BOY 2: And I don't know anything about Captain America other than he's awesome.

NARRATOR 1: All right. Clearly we have a lot of work to do.

NARRATOR 2: And that is what this show is about! IT'S AWESOME!

NARRATOR 1: Part One: Historical Context.

NARRATOR 2: Unnecessary! Skip it! We're just diving in!

NARRATOR 1: Superheroes originated in the aftermath of World War 2, when they were patriotic symbols to fight the Nazis.

NARRATOR 2: Who cares? Moving on!

PART 1: BATMAN

NARRATOR 1: Fine. Part 1—The Batman.

NARRATOR 2: Or, a billionaire white dude is the victim of crime and uses his fortune to scare the hell out of everyone else in his insane quest to make the world safe for other billionaires.

NARRATOR 1: You may be familiar with his Dark Knight incarnation, but there have been many Batmans. Many, many Batmans. In fact, the best one was this guy—1960s TV Batman.

(BATMAN and ROBIN, in old-timey costumes, run in.)

BATMAN: Well, chum, this looks like a job for the Dynamic Duo.

ROBIN: I was hoping I could wear pants. Do we have pants I could wear?

BATMAN: Have no fear, good friend. Your legs are a credit to your gender.

ROBIN: Thanks. That's not awkward.

BATMAN: Is your suit riding up? Mine rides up.

ROBIN: You gotta wear the right kind of underwear.

BATMAN: That just slows me down, Boy Wonder. Come, I'll need your acrobatic assistance to try something out.

ROBIN: What are we going to do?

BATMAN: Luckily, my utility belt is equipped with the Batsuit-Un-Wedgifier.

(He produces a long pole-like device.)

ROBIN: I'm ready, Batman! Though it might take all of my strength!

BATMAN: Fear not, Robin. Your extensive calisthenics will provide you with all the strength and flexibility you need.

ROBIN: Holy Fishing Expedition, Batman!

BATMAN: You stand behind me here and—

NARRATOR 2: Can we actually get to the crime fighting?

NARRATOR 1: I was getting to that.

(Batman holds a rolled-up piece of paper.)

BATMAN: Wait! There's no time. I'll just have to keep my concentration away from my personal discomfort. It's a riddle from that Capricious Cavalier, the Riddler.

ROBIN: Holy Holy Things, Batman! What does it say?

BATMAN: It's series of pictographs.

ROBIN: Holy crap!

BATMAN: Robin. Though we are pressed on all sides by super-criminals, if we start using poor language, they've already beaten us.

ROBIN: I was referring to the Crappie. A kind of fish.

BATMAN: My apologies, Boy Wonder. I should have known I could trust you.

ROBIN: So what do the pictographs mean? If only we had the Batcomputer to tell us.

BATMAN: We have no need of the Batcomputer as I have already deciphered this riddle with my very own brain.

ROBIN: Holy crap!

BATMAN: Another fish?

ROBIN: Sure.

BATMAN: Clearly, there's a picture of a kitten, followed by three eyes and an alien spacecraft. Quite obviously, the Riddler is planning on striking Fort Knox.

ROBIN: Oh. Let's take a taxi there!

BATMAN: I'm afraid it's rush hour and we would likely be stuck with a cabbie who doesn't speak English.

ROBIN: Holy Cab!

BATMAN: Luckily, my muscles are warm and loose and my suit breathes well. We bat-jog there.

ROBIN: Brilliant idea, Batman! And we can get some exercise. Let's go!

(*They jog off.*)

NARRATOR 2: I wish more superheroes would jog to crime.

NARRATOR 1: Now you might be thinking that being a superhero is a job for a man.

(CLARK enters.)

CLARK: Not just any man. A super...man.

NARRATOR 2: We're not ready for you yet.

CLARK: All right. I'll just be over here using my x-ray vision to make you uncomfortable.

NARRATOR 2: What?

CLARK: Heh-heh-heh.

(He exits.)

NARRATOR 2: Does he make you feel weird?

NARRATOR 1: Oh yeah.

CLARK: *(Off:)* I can still see you. Heh-heh-heh.

PART 2. WONDER WOMAN

NARRATOR 2: But there are also superheroes who are ladies. Such as...Wonder Woman!

(WONDER WOMAN enters in bathrobe.)

WONDER WOMAN: Hey. I'm here to fight crime.

NARRATOR 2: Hey [actor's name], what's going on?

WONDER WOMAN: What?

NARRATOR 2: Why aren't you wearing the costume?

WONDER WOMAN: I had breakfast today so uh... I'm not really comfortable fitting into the leotard.

NARRATOR 1: Don't worry about it.

NARRATOR 2: Whoah whoah whoah, what about realism?! We all know that superheroines fight crime wearing skin-tight outfits! Otherwise, the terrorists win!

WONDER WOMAN: It's a little sexist, actually. The dudes don't wear skin-tight outfits.

(Batman runs on.)

BATMAN: Actually...

NARRATOR 2: We don't need you right now, Batman.

BATMAN: Good. 'Cause I've got some things to work on. Luckily, I am in peak physical condition. As you can clearly see.

(He jogs off.)

WONDER WOMAN: Isn't there a way we could have better costumes?

NARRATOR 2: This totally ruins my vision for you. There is nothing sexist about this, all right! You fight crime wearing a leotard and come from a mythical island where scantily dressed ladies hang out all day. It's feminism.

(BLACK CANARY enters in a bathrobe.)

BLACK CANARY: Hey I'm Black Canary. I'm not sure what my powers are, but I'm having the same issue.

(WHITE QUEEN enters from the opposite direction, also wearing a bathrobe.)

WHITE QUEEN: Yeah. Me too.

NARRATOR 2: Black Canary and White Queen! What are you two doing here, seeing as how one of you is a DC hero and the other one is a Marvel villain?

BOY 2: I'm getting confused now.

NARRATOR 2: Shut up. Go get in costume.

BLACK CANARY: Um...my parents are here for the show so uh...no.

WHITE QUEEN: And my costume appears to be a teddy.

NARRATOR 2: Yes. Yes it is.

WHITE QUEEN: Am I using my mutant powers to keep the costume on?

NARRATOR 2: Probably. Look—you are wearing the revealing outfit because you're evil, and it reveals your evilness. And you, Black Canary, are wearing a revealing outfit because you're a hero, and it shows your heroic sides. All over the place. Your ample heroic sides.

NARRATOR 1: All right, we're done with this.

(HULK enters, wearing a bathrobe.)

HULK: Hulk not comfortable showing this much skin. Rarrrrhg!

NARRATOR 2: All right fine! Ditch the costumes. Wear whatever makes you comfortable!

WONDER WOMAN: Thank you.

(She leaves.)

HULK: Hulk smash gender stereotypes!

(Hulk, Black Canary and the White Queen exit.)

NARRATOR 2: Any-way, where were we?

NARRATOR 1: We were learning about sexism in comics.

NARRATOR 2: No, I mean in the story.

NARRATOR 1: Oh, we were at Wonder Woman's origin.

NARRATOR 2: Right. So on the Amazonian island of Themiskyra, there was a great princess. Diana.

(Wonder Woman enters in full-coverage pajamas.)

Seriously?

WONDER WOMAN: You said whatever makes me comfortable.

NARRATOR 2: And on the islands were all the other Amazons.

> *(AMAZONS enter, wearing business suits, or other suitably non-sexy outfits.)*

Really? Amazons? This is what you're wearing on your island in the Mediterranean?

AMAZONIAN QUEEN: Diana. You're willing to give up your place here to help out losers?

WONDER WOMAN: Yes, Mother. I can't help it. I love the mortals.

AMAZONIAN QUEEN: Why?

WONDER WOMAN: Um...no reason really. Can't think of one. But also we have really poor cell phone service here.

AMAZONIAN QUEEN: We're working on that.

WONDER WOMAN: I want to see the world!

AMAZONIAN QUEEN: All right. Fine. Whatever. I've got other daughters.

WONDER WOMAN: Great!

AMAZONIAN QUEEN: And put some clothes on.

WONDER WOMAN: Stop telling me what to do, Mom! This is what all the mortal girls are wearing!

> *(She storms off.)*

NARRATOR 2: Wonder Woman takes on a secret identity, Diana Prince.

NARRATOR 1: She's not really getting the whole name thing.

NARRATOR 2: And takes a job as a lady secretary.

WONDER WOMAN: My womanly powers will best be used typing and filing!

NARRATOR 2: For a handsome boss. A dreamily handsome boss.

(*BOSS enters.*)

BOSS: Miss Prince, I'm going to need those files filed pronto. We've got a big case coming up.

WONDER WOMAN: Yes, sir.

BOSS: And would it kill you to wear some more makeup? I'm running a business here, not a commune.

WONDER WOMAN: Great Hera! I think I love him! But will he be able to accept a powerful woman as a girlfriend? And what if I can't cook!? This is more dangerous than a seven-headed hydra and... (*She breaks character.*) I'm sorry this is just...

NARRATOR 1: Yeah I know. Actually—Wonder Woman was a feminist at the very beginning, but then DC freaked out and made her into a secretary in magic underwear later on.

NARRATOR 2: You're ruining this!

WONDER WOMAN: This is just—

NARRATOR 2: And remember you have super-powers until you are tied up by a man. In which case you're helpless.

WONDER WOMAN: What? Batman doesn't have to deal with this.

BOSS: Miss Prince! I don't pay you for gossip! Now I know, as a female, you're required to do a certain amount of idle chatter, but I'm running a business here!

WONDER WOMAN: I think I know what to do!

BOSS: Yes, you should. I only explained it to you three times—you wear some high heels, and then do the—

(BAM! Wonder Woman punches him in the face.)

NARRATOR 1: And she killed him.

WONDER WOMAN: What?

NARRATOR 1: You can lift a 50,000-pound boulder over your head, what do you think happens when you punch a guy in the face?

WONDER WOMAN: Oh darn it. Well, he probably deserved to die.

NARRATOR 2: This is not what happens in Wonder Woman's origin story!

NARRATOR 1: Here's something else to learn about comics: Every five years, they rewrite the entire history of every character and change things. It's called ret-conning.

WONDER WOMAN: But now I'm a murderer!

NARRATOR 1: No worries. You're a princess from a foreign country. You've got diplomatic immunity.

WONDER WOMAN: Sweet!

NARRATOR 1: And so Wonder Woman fought her way through the business world, killing all the sexists.

NARRATOR 2: What?

NARRATOR 1: It took her a while.

WONDER WOMAN: I AM WOMAN! HEAR ME PUNCH YOU IN THE FACE!

(BOSS 2, BOSS 3, and BOSS 4 enter in opposite parts of the stage.)

BOSS 2: No one's gonna watch women's soccer unless they wear tighter outfits.

(BAM! Wonder Woman punches him in the face, killing him.)

BOSS 3: So I've got this great idea for a restaurant: Hooters.

(BAM! Punched. Dead.)

BOSS 4: *(Calling to a Secretary:)* Hey Sweetheart get me a coffee, will ya?

WONDER WOMAN: She's not your sweetheart!

(BAM! Wonder Woman punches him in the face, killing him.)

(SECRETARY enters.)

SECRETARY: Actually, we're married...we kind of do a little thing where I pretend to be the secretary... Keeps our marriage interesting. Or it did. Before you killed him.

WONDER WOMAN: Oh. My bad.

NARRATOR 1: And she lived happily ever after. And was elected President. And helped girls feel comfortable with their body image.

(Wonder Woman exits.)

NARRATOR 2: Wow. Yep.

GIRL: When does Wonder Woman get her own movie?

NARRATOR 2: Um... Pretty sure Warner Brothers doesn't think anyone will go see a movie starring a girl.

NARRATOR 1: Like *Hunger Games*. Or *Divergent*. Or *Frozen*. Or *Inside Out*.

(She keeps naming movies with female protagonists.)

PART 3: SUPERMAN

NARRATOR 2: Moving on! The last of the three great heroes in the DC Comics universe:

(Clark enters, showing a little bit of his suit beneath his clothes.)

Aquaman!

(AQUAMAN runs on.)

AQUAMAN: Woo! If there are any crimes happening in the water, I'm your man!

CLARK: Whoah, hold on.

AQUAMAN: Let's say someone is stealing a giant pearl—from the ocean—I can be there!

CLARK: Aquaman? Seriously? I can basically do everything you can do.

AQUAMAN: Can you talk to fish?

CLARK: I can eat fish. I fry them up with my laser vision and then eat them. You can listen to their screams.

AQUAMAN: What about flying fish? If there were like flying piranhas or something that would be really cool.

CLARK: There are no flying piranhas.

AQUAMAN: What about a Sharknado? That would be pretty awesome if I could control a Sharknado.

NARRATOR 2: All right—I was kidding, Aquaman, you're the worst hero ever, get off the stage.

AQUAMAN: I'm gonna talk to my only friends, the trout!

NARRATOR 1: Hey what do fish talk about anyway?

AQUAMAN: They mostly listen.

(He runs off, crying.)

NARRATOR 2: All right then. It's time for Superman. An illegal alien taking American jobs.

NARRATOR 1: Once upon a time, on the planet Krypton.

(JOR-EL runs in with LARA.)

(Distant explosions.)

JOR-EL: We're all going to die! Let's put a baby in a rocket!

LARA: What?

JOR-EL: There's no time for logical thought! I've built a baby-sized rocket which will survive the trip to a distant planet with no ill effects whatsoever!

LARA: Why didn't you make it big enough for us?

JOR-EL: Woman, I told you there was no time for logical thought! Quick, bring me Kal-El!

LARA: No. You're insane.

JOR-EL: That's what they said when I said I wanted to make the rocket only big enough for a baby. But who's laughing now?! Ha ha ha. Seriously—hand me our only child, this is probably going to work.

LARA: That's what you said about our last son.

JOR-EL: And I'm sure he's doing great out there in space by himself with no food.

LARA: I don't know, Jor-El.

JOR-EL: NO ONE'S GOING TO STOP ME FROM PUTTING A BABY IN A ROCKET! THIS IS A GOOD IDEA!

LARA: You're going to look really dumb if the planet doesn't blow up.

JOR-EL: Lara. I need you to trust me. This time the planet's going to blow up for sure.

LARA: I should've married your brother.

JOR-EL: Give me the baby!

LARA: Fine, but I'm not making another one!

JOR-EL: Sweet! Also—I've built a dog-sized rocket for our dog.

(They head off.)

NARRATOR 1: And so, like the greatest parents on Krypton, they placed their infant son in an untested rocket and sent him to Earth.

NARRATOR 2: Question: He's an alien from a distant planet?

NARRATOR 1: Yes.

NARRATOR 2: And yet, he basically looks like a white dude from Kansas?

NARRATOR 1: Yeah. What a coincidence!

NARRATOR 2: Like, why wouldn't he be like two inches tall, or made out of silicon, or be like a weird fish-type thing?

(Aquaman enters.)

AQUAMAN: Ooh!

NARRATOR 2: Shut up. You can only talk to Earth fish anyway.

AQUAMAN: Dang it.

NARRATOR 1: Stop asking intelligent questions! Anyway, Superman grows up and totally doesn't abuse his powers or accidentally kill his foster parents or DO ANYTHING WRONG AT ALL.

CLARK: Can you imagine what it was like being 12 with X-ray vision? One word for you: Enlightening. And scary. And not as cool as you might think.

NARRATOR 2: Can you imagine a three-year-old that can lift an airplane throwing a temper tantrum?

NARRATOR 1: Yeah, we're just gonna skip his childhood as that makes even less sense than the whole rest of this story.

NARRATOR 2: Anyway, there was one defining moment in his young life —

(Clark enters, with football helmet.)

MOM: Clark?

CLARK: Yeah, Mom?

MOM: What did I tell you about playing on the football team?

CLARK: Hey, I toned it down. Plus, chicks totally dig me now.

MOM: You scored 43 touchdowns last game.

CLARK: I thought I would take it easy.

MOM: The other team started running away from you, son.

CLARK: I'm not your son! I'm adopted! My real parents would let me play football! And put me into a rocket by myself. I'm alone, don't you get it?! Dominating every sport in high school is my way of dealing with my abandonment issues!

MOM: Shhhh! There are...people here to see you.

CLARK: What people? College scouts? I'm going to Notre Dame, I've already decided. Heisman Trophies, here I come.

(Two INS AGENTS enter.)

INS AGENT 1: Hi there, Clark.

INS AGENT 2: What's up, Slugger?

MOM: Clark is a little busy right now.

INS AGENT 1: Oh sure. We understand.

INS AGENT 2: We'll make this quick.

INS AGENT 1: We're from the INS.

INS AGENT 2: Immigration and Naturalization Services.

CLARK: I don't care about your Acronyms.

INS AGENT 1: We don't either.

INS AGENT 2: But we have reason to believe that you...are an illegal alien.

MOM: Ha ha. Ha ha. That's crazy. Clark is just like us. Except different.

INS AGENT 1: And we're pretty sure you're going to take American jobs. We're gonna need to see a birth certificate—

CLARK: Or what?! What are you gonna do about it! I'm a star high school athlete! No laws apply to me!

MOM: Settle down, Clark.

CLARK: Racists!

MOM: All right—

INS AGENT 2: I'm afraid we're gonna have to deport you.

MOM: No! Don't take my baby! He's just a little boy, don't you understand?! His real parents didn't want him!

INS AGENT 1: Come along, Clark. We're going to put you on a plane back to your home country.

INS AGENT 2: We figure it's Canada.

CLARK: Hey you know something cool? I have laser eye beams. So I can basically kill you by looking at you funny.

NARRATOR 1: Can we pause for a second? Who the heck came up with his powers?!

(MAN 1 and 2 enter, excited.)

MAN 1: He can leap tall buildings in a single bound!

MAN 2: Dude, he can fly, why does he need to leap over buildings?

MAN 1: He's faster than a locomotive!

MAN 2: Locomotives are like thirty miles an hour. He can fly. Why aren't you getting that?

MAN 1: And he's really strong!

MAN 2: Like how strong?

MAN 1: He can rip like four phone books in half with his bare hands! And pick up heavy rocks and suitcases!

MAN 2: How about he can lift the moon?

MAN 1: Sounds good. And he has X-ray vision.

MAN 2: And heat vision!

MAN 1: And frosty breath.

MAN 2: And he's invulnerable. Like you can shoot bullets in his eyes.

MAN 1: And he's got like super-hearing!

MAN 2: And extendable arms.

MAN 1: And wi-fi!

MAN 2: And he can change his feet into tires!

MAN 1: And he's like a chameleon!

MAN 2: And he's got like scissor teeth that can cut through anything like scissors!

MAN 1: And he can talk to fish!

(Aquaman enters.)

AQUAMAN: Whoah! Whoah. Hold on. That's my thing.

MAN 1: Yes. We've gone too far.

(They exit.)

CLARK: Where was I? Oh yes, I was casually threatening you with instant death.

INS AGENT 1: You don't scare us!

(Clark uses his laser eye beams to incinerate INS Agent 2.)

CLARK: Eye beam attack!

INS AGENT 2: Ah! I'm being incinerated!

(INS Agent 2 dies.)

Fizzle. Fizzle.

INS AGENT 1: Okay, now you scare me. You can stay.

CLARK: Sweet!

MOM: Oh my boy! My sweet boy!

CLARK: Hug?

MOM: No thanks.

NARRATOR 1: And that's how he became a champion of truth, justice, and the American way. By destroying those who would stop him.

NARRATOR 2: Moving on! We've addressed the holy trinity of DC Superheroes.

BOY 2: From Washington?

NARRATOR 2: No. DC stands for...something. And they're one brand of comics. And Marvel stands for something else, and they're another brand of comics. And the two universes never touch! Ever!

BOY 2: What happens if you cross the streams?

NARRATOR 1: Everything blows up. Imagine the universe is a plastic bag, and then you turn that bag...inside-out. That's what happens.

BOY 2: So everything falls out of it?

NARRATOR 2: No it just—it's not pleasant, that's all.

NARRATOR 1: Actually, Marvel and DC did some cross-over events in the 80s, Spiderman versus Batman, Superman fought the Hulk—

NARRATOR 2: Nobody needs to learn knowledge or facts from a girl, okay?! We get enough of that in school!

PART 4: THE AVENGERS

NARRATOR 1: Fine. Moving on to the Marvel side of the aisle. Or the people who make good movies.

NARRATOR 2: Whoah. Take that back.

NARRATOR 1: They're just better. I mean, deal with it.

NARRATOR 2: Have you seen *The Dark Knight*?

NARRATOR 1: Yeah, I had nightmares for weeks. Anyway— On to the best superhero team of all time—

NARRATOR 2: Justice League.

NARRATOR 1: Avengers.

(Aquaman enters.)

AQUAMAN: X-Men.

(He leaves.)

NARRATOR 1: Avengers! Now, if you're like this child over here and aren't familiar with the Avengers—let's just say that there have been many, many members of the Avengers. Legendary heroes such as Doctor Druid, Swordsman, Mantis, Moondragon, and the Two-Gun Kid.

NARRATOR 2: I don't know who those people are.

NARRATOR 1: Most of them were killed fairly quickly. They were not good heroes. Look, there have been like 900 members of the Avengers over the years—there's a high turnover rate.

NARRATOR 2: Sometimes people go insane and become villains.

NARRATOR 1: But basically it's just a job. I mean they have a regular office.

NARRATOR 2: So let's take a look at a typical day at Avengers Headquarters when no one is threating to destroy the earth!

(Plinky office theme music plays.)

(The Avengers enter, in street clothes. NATASHA/BLACK WIDOW mans the phones as a receptionist.)

(HAWKEYE talks into the confessional.)

HAWKEYE: I'm gonna ask her out. Pretty sure today's the day. Or not. If I chicken out, but um...you know, you don't get to be a hero without taking some risks. People said the whole bow thing wasn't going to work out for me, and check me now. I may not be the most powerful Avenger, but um...you know... I pull my weight. Sometimes. And yeah, I know, she's the only girl on the team, so everybody's hitting on her. And, yes, her name is Black Widow, which suggests that she will kill me with poison after she mates with me, but...that's a risk I'm willing to take.

(The phone rings.)

NATASHA: Avengers Headquarters. Natasha speaking. How may I direct your call? No I'm sorry—Iron Man usually doesn t come in 'til 10. But I've got Hawkeye here and... She hung up. *(Looking into the "camera":)* Most annoying in the office? Hands down: Thor. He's all like, "I'm a God," which is technically true, but I don't care if you're immortal or not, when you empty the printer, you need to replace the paper. I mean, it doesn't take God-like strength to reach down, open the cabinet, and put some more paper in there, you know? Like—oh that's so *beneath* him, you know? "The Son of Odin kneels to no one! Least of all this printer!" Such a jerk.

(Hawkeye comes over.)

HAWKEYE: I know, right? And don't get me started on Captain America. Total power trip.

NATASHA: Hawkeye, I'm doing my confessional right now.

HAWKEYE: Oh, right. Right. Sorry.

(THOR approaches with hammer.)

THOR: Pull my hammer.

NATASHA: No.

THOR: Do it. Pull my hammer. If you dare.

NATASHA: I really don't think this is funny.

THOR: Only the worthy may pull my hammer. I'll just set this here.

(He sets his hammer down, sits next to Natasha.)

Are we speaking into the magic box?

NATASHA: Yes, it's the video cameras—they're doing a documentary.

(Thor stares into the "camera.")

THOR: Behold Thor, God of Thunder. You want to see the Gun Show? It's about time for the Gun Show!

NATASHA: Thor!

THOR: Pull my hammer.

NATASHA: You're so juvenile.

THOR: Ha ha ha ha ha. What about you, Hawkeye? Feeling lucky?

HAWKEYE: Thor, don't you have some faxing to do?

THOR: Speak to me not of faxing! There will be no faxing from now on!

NATASHA: What did you do to the fax machine?

THOR: It was possessed by a demon. I have liberated it. With violence.

NATASHA: Oh man did you break another fax machine?

THOR: I saved all of us. You may show your appreciation by pulling my hammer.

HAWKEYE: All right. I'm going back to work. There's a lot of applications coming in to replace Iron Man when he goes on paternity leave.

THOR: The God of Thunder needs no paternity leave!

NATASHA: Hey Thor—I know you're a God and all, but I have a little question: exactly how many people worship you?

THOR: Depends on whether or not they've seen... The Gun Show!

NATASHA: All right.

(STEVE rushes in, in his Captain America costume.)

STEVE: Heads up everyone! We've got a robbery in progress at Seventh Avenue and Market Street! Avengers Assemble!

(BRUCE enters.)

BRUCE: Steve, come on.

STEVE: This is a live one!

BRUCE: I'm not gonna Hulk-out for this. Robbery? Is there like mind control involved?

STEVE: This is pretty frightening! We're gonna need back-up! I'm going to call the West Coast Avengers!

HAWKEYE: Steve. It's like six in the morning there. Chill out for a second.

STEVE: What?

HAWKEYE: Don't you think this is a little below our pay grade?

STEVE: We're doing broken windows policing now. If we ignore the small crimes, pretty soon we'll have super crimes.

BRUCE: Look, I'd love to help out, but I just bought these clothes.

NARRATOR 2: Side note: How does Bruce Banner shop for clothes, anyway?

(Bruce steps to the side as a SALESGIRL enters.)

SALESGIRL: Oh this looks fantastic on you!

BRUCE: Yeah. So do these like, breathe?

SALESGIRL: Oh sure. It's a cotton blend.

BRUCE: Right. But let's say I'm planning on working out a lot—getting pumped—

SALESGIRL: It would still look good.

BRUCE: Basically, when I rip out of these pants, are they gonna give me full coverage? And also, can they turn purple? I have powerful buttocks. They need to be enclosed.

(Salesgirl stares angrily at him and leaves.)

(Lights up on TONY, talking into the "camera.")

TONY: Yeah, I mean, I love Steve like a brother. But he's so gung ho, you know? Every time he's out on the patrol, I get a call.

(GIRL 3 enters.)

STEVE: Citizen!

GIRL 3: Oh my gosh are you Captain America?

STEVE: I noticed you jaywalking back there.

GIRL 3: What?

STEVE: You crossed the street at a place other than a designated crosswalk.

GIRL 3: Oh.

STEVE: I'm gonna need to take you down.

GIRL 3: Can I get an autograph first?

STEVE: No autographs for evildoers.

(He drags her off. Maybe fights her.)

TONY: Yeah, so it's hard to take him seriously sometimes. I mean, if you're not having any fun saving the world, why bother right? Anyway, so we're doing the fall membership drive—which is just really brings out the crazy.

(Thor approaches.)

THOR: Pull my hammer.

TONY: Thor. I'm in the middle of this.

NATASHA: I think I would like another woman to join.

TONY: Oh no here we go with the gender parity talk again. We have one woman, do we really need any more?

NATASHA: Maybe we could have a person of color too?

BRUCE: Um, hello? I'm a person of color.

NATASHA: You know what I mean.

TONY: Whoah, whoah, whoah, we asked that guy to join. What's his name, Black Falcon?

HAWKEYE: It's just Falcon. There's no Black in it.

TONY: I thought it was Black Falcon.

HAWKEYE: You're not White Iron Man.

TONY: There's a Black Panther. I know there's a dude named Black Panther.

STEVE: He sounds like a villain.

(*Thor is checking his cell phone.*)

HAWKEYE: Can we just do the interviews please? Thor, get off your phone.

THOR: I'm not on my phone. If I was on my phone I would crush it, mortal.

HAWKEYE: Stop updating your Twitter feed then.

THOR: I need more followers. I'm offering life advice.

HAWKEYE: How can you offer life advice? You can't die!

THOR: I have noticed you are not following me on Twitter. Jealous?

HAWKEYE: I have Instagram, not Twitter.

NATASHA: Can we just start the interview process please?!

STEVE: Good idea. Let's do this! Avengers Assemble!

TONY: Dude, we're all right here.

STEVE: To the comfy chairs!

(*The Avengers seat themselves as JENNIFER enters.*)

JENNIFER: Hey there, my name's Jennifer Walters.

TONY: Awesome. What do you got for us, babe?

NATASHA: Would you stop it? That was sexist.

TONY: I didn't call her Sweetcheeks. I could've called her Sweetcheeks and I didn't.

THOR: High five!

NATASHA: No! No high fives!

THOR: The God of Thunder will determine his own high fives!

TONY: Just a question: how do you feel about wearing a leather bodysuit? Just throwing ideas out there.

JENNIFER: I don't really feel comfortable with that.

TONY: She's out!

HAWKEYE: Can you show us your powers?

JENNIFER: Sure I can. But first I just want to...here's my resume...

(She hands out copies of her resumes to people.)

THOR: I don't read.

JENNIFER: Oh. Um...

THOR: I could read, but I choose not to.

JENNIFER: Anyway, you can see—I interned with the Fantastic Four, and I had a team-up with Spiderman for a while, he's one of my references on page two.

TONY: I'm sorry, what is your power?

JENNIFER: I'm known as the She-Hulk.

BRUCE: Oh man. No way. We already got one!

JENNIFER: You can't use two hulks?

BRUCE: The position is filled! I'm getting angry! You won't like me when I'm angry!

JENNIFER: That's the difference between us. I'm in control of my mind when I Hulk out, unlike a typical man.

BRUCE: Whoah! Arrrrhg!

TONY: Settle down, Greenie.

THOR: You want to pull my hammer?

HAWKEYE: Thor! That is not appropriate!

TONY: So is the bodysuit out then?

NATASHA: This is a really poisonous work environment, Jennifer. Maybe you should join the X-Men or something.

JENNIFER: They only let mutants in.

NATASHA: You're not a mutant?

JENNIFER: No, I mutated, but I'm not a mutant.

BRUCE: Hey where do you shop, by the way?

JENNIFER: Spandex. Really works. Expands.

BRUCE: Huh.

JENNIFER: Very form-fitting, though.

BRUCE: Yeah. That might not...uh...be the best choice for me. I don't want to be the obscene Hulk, know what I mean?

TONY: All right, look, we're probably full of strong guys right now. We're really looking for someone with super-speed or laser powers or um...

HAWKEYE: Telepathy.

TONY: That would be way cool. So we'll call you.

JENNIFER: Maybe you should call him He-Hulk.

(She walks out.)

THOR: I liked her.

(An Alarm Sounds!)

(Steve rushes to check something.)

STEVE: Emergency! We've got tax fraud at a downtown law firm! Avengers Assemble!

(He runs out.)

TONY: Yeah...anybody up for karaoke?

(They leave, except for Hawkeye.)

HAWKEYE: Now's my chance. "Islands in the Stream" duet. Wish me luck.

(Steve runs back in.)

STEVE: Hawkeye! Come on!

(Hawkeye grits his teeth sadly.)

HAWKEYE: Duty calls.

STEVE: Let's put some arrows through some paperwork!

(They run off.)

NARRATOR 1: Earth's mightiest heroes, indeed.

PART 5: X-MEN

NARRATOR 2: And now's time to explore the most popular side of the Marvel universe: The mutants.

(MOM and DAD enter.)

MOM 2: Hey Jim, have you noticed that Angelica is acting weird lately?

DAD 2: Ah dang it. She's 15. She acts weird all the time. When I was her age I was completely normal. And a boy.

(ANGELICA enters.)

ANGELICA: Mom and Dad. Can I talk to you for a second?

DAD 2: Hold on. Let me mentally prepare myself.

MOM 2: Jim.

DAD 2: Silence, woman! *(He meditates a little bit.)* Ommm... IT'S NOT WORKING, DANG IT!

MOM 2: Go ahead Angelica. What do you need to tell us?

ANGELICA: Okay, um...here goes: you've probably noticed, or maybe you haven't, that I've always been a little bit...different.

DAD 2: Oh yeah. Totally.

MOM 2: You're not different honey, you're just odd.

DAD 2: Total freak show.

MOM 2: Jim!

DAD 2: What? I'm just speaking my mind here. I can't do that anymore? Is that what we've come to now?! So much for freedom of speech! Sorry, honey. We're pretty sure you're going to grow out of this phase.

ANGELICA: Right but um...this is a difference that I'm probably not going to grow out of.

DAD 2: Okay.

ANGELICA: It's something I was born with.

MOM: Honey, we love you as much as is legally required. You can tell us anything.

DAD: And we will still love you. Although we may remove you from our Christmas card list.

ANGELICA: Okay. *(She takes a deep breath.)* So...what I need to tell you is...gosh this is hard...

MOM: It's okay. We've known for a long time.

ANGELICA: I'm...

MOM: Gay.

ANGELICA: What?

MOM: Gay?

ANGELICA: That's not what I was going to say!

DAD: Are you sure?

ANGELICA: Yes! Is that what you thought?!

MOM: Well you did play with G.I. Joe that one time.

ANGELICA: That doesn't make me gay!

DAD: Coulda fooled me.

ANGELICA: Dad!

DAD: Oh yeah—I totally called this one when you were like four. Remember honey?

MOM: Yes.

ANGELICA: Four!?

DAD: I was like, "Hey, 10 bucks she's gay!" In fact, I wrote it down.

ANGELICA: I'm not gay!

DAD: I also said you would deny it.

ANGELICA: I'm a mutant!

MOM: What?

DAD: Seriously?

ANGELICA: I am a mutant, okay? I'm a mutant. People will hate me because I'm different and better than them. I'm going to go join Professor Charles Xavier's school for Gifted Youngsters. And you can't stop me!

MOM: I don't believe this! You just think you're a mutant because it's cool all of a sudden!

DAD: Did the internet make you do this? Did you find this on the internet?

MOM: It was those movies that made being a mutant look cool, wasn't it? Well let me tell you, missy, being a mutant isn't all fighting giant robots and being hated, all right? And those costumes won't even look good on you! You don't have the hips for them!

ANGELICA: I'm not wearing a costume!

DAD: How are we going to tell our friends?! What are they going to say! Hey we heard your daughter is a mutant! Ha ha ha ha! I'm gonna have to fight so many people.

MOM: No daughter of mine is a mutant!

DAD: Hey what's your power anyway, is it something cool?

ANGELICA: I can talk to fish.

DAD: Aw man.

(Aquaman enters.)

AQUAMAN: Whoah. WHOAH! My thing! That is MY thing!

ANGELICA: But I have other cooler powers besides that. I can levitate fish too.

DAD: Aw geez.

MOM: You're not our daughter anymore! Go live with your mutant friends in a big mansion in upstate New York! Have fun hanging out with Hugh Jackman and Halle Berry and other super-attractive people!

DAD: Hey that sounds nice.

MOM: I know, right?

(They exit.)

NARRATOR 2: So what is it really like at the X-Men school?

(PROFESSOR CHARLES XAVIER enters.)

PROFESSOR X: So how's your research paper coming on the Civil War?

STUDENT: Um... I've done preliminary research.

PROFESSOR X: Have you?

STUDENT: Well uh... I've thought about it.

PROFESSOR X: Really?

(Professor X puts his fingers to his temple.)

STUDENT: Okay, I haven't thought about it actually, but I've considered thinking about it.

PROFESSOR X: That's not what your brain says. You spent seven hours last night playing *Call of Duty.*

STUDENT: Right uh...but...

PROFESSOR X: I'm going to erase the motor skills necessary to play that video game.

STUDENT: Aw man.

(WOLVERINE enters.)

WOLVERINE: Professor!

PROFESSOR X: What is it, Logan?

WOLVERINE: Magneto's attacking New York!

PROFESSOR X: Is he? Or is this an elaborate deception to trick me into going into a dark room so a number of you can leap into the air and declare, "Happy Birthday Professor." I see right through you. You might as well come out now. I know your hearts aren't in this, anyway. And thanks for the gift card to Best Buy, that's going to come in really handy, Cyclops.

NARRATOR 1: Being a student of Professor X, not as fun as it sounds.

PART 6: WOLVERINE

NARRATOR 1: And now it's time for Wolverine—the crazy psychopath that we all love to love.

NARRATOR 2: Wolverine isn't one of those lame-o heroes from the 1960s who were all into saving people's lives and other loser stuff.

NARRATOR 1: The cover of the first issue of his comic book is literally him standing on top of a mountain of corpses.

NARRATOR 2: Awesome.

NARRATOR 1: That's not awesome. Is he supposed to be a role model?

NARRATOR 2: Yes.

NARRATOR 1: How?

NARRATOR 2: Let's say you're attacked by an army. You kill them all. It's simple. Anyway, Wolverine is hard-core, and we're about to have a hard-core story.

WOLVERINE: Heck yes.

NARRATOR 2: This ain't no Disney movie, folks!

NARRATOR 1: Actually, um...

NARRATOR 2: What?

NARRATOR 1: Didn't you hear? Disney bought Marvel.

NARRATOR 2: What?

(She takes out her phone.)

NARRATOR 1: Check it out. Wikipedia. 2009.

NARRATOR 2: No!

NARRATOR 1: They also got *Star Wars*.

WOLVERINE: Whoah, hold on. What's going on?

NARRATOR 1: You've been bought by Disney.

WOLVERINE: They're not gonna change anything, are they?

NARRATOR 1: Probably not.

(Two DISNEY EXECs come in.)

DISNEY EXEC 1: Listen, we love you!

DISNEY EXEC 2: We love you so much! In fact I heart you.

WOLVERINE: What's going on?

DISNEY EXEC 1: I did notice that um...you smoke cigars.

WOLVERINE: Yeah.

DISNEY EXEC 1: We can't endorse that. It doesn't make you a good role model.

WOLVERINE: First, I have a healing factor. Second, I kill like a hundred people an hour and you're worried about me smoking?

DISNEY EXEC 2: Right. About that. We have some out-of-the-box ideas for your next film. You're going to love them!

NARRATOR 1: And here we go! The Disneyfication of Wolverine!

(Perhaps a castle is brought in. If not, Wolverine can sit in a medieval stool of some kind. He stares longingly into space.)

(Disney-type music in the background.)

WOLVERINE: If only I wasn't so different. I have such big dreams and I'm trapped in this tower slash little town slash restrictive society.

(MOTHER enters.)

MOTHER: Logan, please get dressed for dinner. The prince is here to see you. Maybe we'll make a match! I hear wedding bells! La la la.

(She exits.)

WOLVERINE: Whoah. Pause. Time out. What?

DISNEY EXEC 2: Two words: Princess Wolverine. Bring in the dress!

(Disney Exec brings in a fancy dress for Wolverine.)

WOLVERINE: Um...

DISNEY EXEC 2: And let's go.

(Wolverine gets into the fancy dress, clumsily.)

WOLVERINE: Oh Mother! I don't want to marry the prince! I want to go out on my own and explore! Besides, what if I'm not the kind of girl he's looking for? I don't feel pretty. Maybe it's my claws. Or my chest hair.

DISNEY EXEC 2: You don't have chest hair in this version!

WOLVERINE: Pretty sure I do! Fine. Maybe it's my claws. Or the fact that I'm a giant ball of muscle.

DISNEY EXEC 1: We're cool with that.

WOLVERINE: All right then. If only there was some way to escape from this tower slash little town slash restrictive society.

(Magical sound effect.)

What's that?

(WOLVIE, a Talking Animal Companion enters.)*

*(*Ideally, this would be a Wolverine Spirit Animal. If you can't come up with a Wolverine animal costume, use any kind of animal and adjust the lines accordingly.)*

(Wolvie floats in majestically.)

WOLVIE: *(British:)* Greetings.

(Wolvie slips and falls and loses British accent completely.)

Whoops! Didn't see that there! Whoah now! Woo. Well Princess Logan, I bet you're wondering what I'm doing here.

WOLVERINE: Do I kill this thing?

DISNEY EXEC 2: Nope. Nope. No killing.

WOLVERINE: Do I just stab this nightmare with my claws?

DISNEY EXEC 1: This is Wolvie, your Spirit Animal.

WOLVERINE: What?

DISNEY EXEC 1: Market research has shown that Talking Animal Companions are really popular.

DISNEY EXEC 2: And they sell a ton of toys.

DISNEY EXEC 1: Wolvie is goofy! He's high-spirited! He's an outside-the-box commercial tie-in! You'll love him!

WOLVERINE: Like romantically?

DISNEY EXEC 2: Nope. No no no no. No romance. That's not how this works. Wolvie is comic relief. Okay?

DISNEY EXEC 1: You can do this. Remember, your target audience is a five-year-old girl. Okay? Love it. I love what you do. More sparkle, though!

DISNEY EXEC 2: Tons more sparkle. And go!

WOLVERINE: Who are you?

WOLVIE: I'm Wolvie! At least I was before I got here! I don't know what I am, now! But—I got news for ya, kid. We're gonna break out of here!

WOLVERINE: Awesome.

WOLVIE: You want to dance?

WOLVERINE: No.

WOLVIE: You want to sing about it?

WOLVERINE: No.

WOLVIE: You mind if I sing about it?

WOLVERINE: Yes.

DISNEY EXEC 2: Sparkle!

WOLVIE: Because I love dancing! In fact, I've got a theme song.

WOLVERINE: Let's try the door.

WOLVIE: Can I do my dance first?

WOLVERINE: Shut up.

WOLVIE: You can't go that way! There are guards!

(Two guards, MONGO and BRUTUS, enter.)

MONGO: I'm Mongo.

BRUTUS: I'm Brutus.

MONGO & BRUTUS: And we're the guards.

WOLVERINE: You're dead guards.

BRUTUS: What?

(Wolverine charges them.)

WOLVERINE: Die die die die!

MONGO & BRUTUS: Aaaaha! She's killing us! The pain! Aaaaaah...

(Mongo and Brutus are dead.)

WOLVERINE: You comin' Wolvie?

DISNEY EXEC 2: Whoah, pause!

DISNEY EXEC 1: Here's an outside-the-box thought! What if, instead of brutally stabbing the guards, you get past them with clever wordplay?

DISNEY EXEC 2: Or a disguise! We love disguises!

WOLVERINE: Shut up.

NARRATOR 1: Meanwhile, in the great hall.

(A PRINCE enters.)

PRINCE: Well Queen Amidala, I would love to get a look at this lovely daughter of yours. I hear she is quite the beauty. Because all princesses are beautiful.

MOTHER: And she would love to meet you as well, Prince. I'm sure that our two kingdoms will be —

(Wolverine enters, dragging a body with him.)

PRINCE: Oh. Princess Logan!

WOLVERINE: What?

PRINCE: Allow me to introduce myself. I am Prince Wilhelm and may I have the pleasure of this dance?

(Wolverine stabs the Prince with his claws.)

Aaaah.

(He dies.)

WOLVERINE: No.

MOTHER: What are you doing?!

WOLVERINE: I'm pretty sure that was a bad guy.

MOTHER: Well, yeah, probably, but—

WOLVERINE: All right then. I'm leaving this tower slash small town slash restrictive society.

MOTHER: But it's dangerous out there!

WOLVERINE: That's right.

WOLVIE: If there's going to be an adventure, wait for me!

WOLVERINE: Sure.

(Wolverine stabs Wolvie repeatedly.)

WOLVIE: Aaaaahh. Why have you betrayed me? We could've been frieeeeends...aaah... Urk.

WOLVERINE: I don't need friends. I'm an independent princess.

(He leaves.)

DISNEY EXEC 1: Well that was unexpected.

DISNEY EXEC 2: Five-year-old boys liked it.

DISNEY EXEC 1: Okay then. Let's film it.

(They leave.)

NARRATOR 2: That was magical.

NARRATOR 1: Yeah.

NARRATOR 2: I'm gonna need a break! All right then! Let's all think about violence and death and then come back here for Act Two! Wooo! Wooo! This is when you clap.

(Lights down. End of Act I.)

ACT II

(The Narrators enter.)

NARRATOR 2: Are your phones off? Seriously? Everybody got their phone off?

NARRATOR 1: We'll know if you're lying. They light up.

NARRATOR 2: Because this part of the show that's coming up is so mind-blowing that if you were to videotape it and leak it to Comic Con, we'd all be arrested...for being too awesome.

BOY 2: Um...so I have some questions about the stuff in Act One.

NARRATOR 2: Shut up. We're moving on.

GIRL: What if I have questions because I'm a girl?

NARRATOR 1: Okay, look, whoever wrote her lines—they're not funny, okay? Not funny. Girls aren't any dumber than super-intelligent boys.

NARRATOR 2: Yeah.

NARRATOR 1: Taking you a minute to get that one, isn't it? You know why? Because you are not as smart as the average girl.

GIRL: I'm still a little fuzzy on Wolverine's backstory. Like—

NARRATOR 2: No one knows what it is, okay?

BOY 2: I think he was an alien.

NARRATOR 2: How are you ever going to become competent members of society if you can't master the basic facts of superheroes?! Shut up and learn, okay?

BOY 2: Fine. So he was an alien?

NARRATOR 1: Just smile and nod, that's the best way to deal with them.

NARRATOR 2: Yes he was an alien.

PART 7: DR. AND MRS. DOOM

NARRATOR 1: But you know what I've noticed?

NARRATOR 2: No. No I don't.

NARRATOR 1: Why is it that like 80% of the heroes are boys?

NARRATOR 2: Oh here we go again. Why not just accept the fact that male superheroes are so much cooler than female superheroes?

NARRATOR 1: But what about the women behind those heroes? What about the wives of those heroes?

NARRATOR 2: They don't have wives. It's mostly wish-fulfillment. Am I right, guys? Am I right? Who wants to be single forever! Yeah! Keep reading those comic books!

(DR. DOOM enters, triumphantly carrying a device.)

DR. DOOM: I, Victor Von Doom, have embarked upon my most ambitious plan yet. The atom Destabilizer and Matter Reformulator! Ah ha ha ha!

MRS. DOOM: *(Calling, off:)* Sweetheart?

DR. DOOM: Aw dang it.

(He starts hiding the Atom Destablizer.)

What is it, Snookums?

(MRS. DOOM enters.)

MRS. DOOM: I thought I heard gloating laughter in here.

DR. DOOM: No, I um... I was just making a joke to myself.

MRS. DOOM: Uh-huh.

DR. DOOM: About bunnies.

MRS. DOOM: Did you look into private schools for junior?

DR. DOOM: Um... I was gonna get to that.

MRS. DOOM: Did you take the garbage out?

DR. DOOM: I've actually built several robots of myself to do the housework.

MRS. DOOM: Yeah, well they don't work. Just like you.

DR. DOOM: I have a job!

MRS. DOOM: Evil madman isn't a job, honey! When I married you I thought "here was a go-getter!" And my Mom was like, "Oh he's a doctor."

DR. DOOM: I am a doctor!

MRS. DOOM: Your honorary doctorate from Southern Indiana University doesn't count!

DR. DOOM: Yes it does!

MRS. DOOM: Get a job! Okay? That's what you should be doing instead of sitting here wearing an iron mask and building—

(She finds the Atom Destabilizer.)

What is this?

DR. DOOM: Nothing. Please don't touch that.

MRS. DOOM: Is this what you've been doing today? I thought you were working on your resume.

DR. DOOM: Doom needs no resume!

MRS. DOOM: Doom needs a job!

DR. DOOM: Don't you understand? Once I rule the universe, I will spare nothing on you—

MRS. DOOM: Oh here we go with the once I rule the universe talk. You know what, I thought you were just being poetic when we started dating.

DR. DOOM: I was serious. Deadly serious. You see—the Atom Destabilizer—

MRS. DOOM: Is that was this is? I thought this was the Molecule Rearranger.

DR. DOOM: No that project was flawed from the beginning. But this one—this will be my crowning achievement! With this device I will triumph over my enemies at last! Doom will reign supreme! Aha ha ha ha ha!

(Mrs. Doom is staring at him, unimpressed.)

What?

MRS. DOOM: What do you think?

DR. DOOM: I don't know.

MRS. DOOM: In your genius mad scientist brain you can't figure out what I'm thinking?

DR. DOOM: No, that's why I asked you a question.

MRS. DOOM: You have no idea what I'm thinking right now?

DR. DOOM: Well I could build a telepathy device but that's going to take at least a month.

MRS. DOOM: I DON'T WANT YOU TO BUILD A TELEPATHY DEVICE!

DR. DOOM: YOU ALWAYS DO THIS! I'M NOT A MIND READER, WOMAN!

MRS. DOOM: GET A JOB!

DR. DOOM: YOU'RE NOT BEING SUPPORTIVE OF MY DREAMS!

MRS DOOM: GET YOUR BUTT OUT OF YOUR SECRET LAB AND TAKE OUT THE GARBAGE!

DR. DOOM: FINE! IF THAT'S WHAT YOU WANT I'LL TAKE OUT THE GARBAGE! I'LL TAKE OUT ALL THE GARBAGE!

MRS. DOOM: Is that a threat?!

DR. DOOM: DOOM WILL NOT BE CONTROLLED!

MRS. DOOM: YES DOOM WILL!

(They stare at each other.)

DR. DOOM: All right I'll take out the garbage but then I need to work on my Atom Destabilizer.

MRS. DOOM: First you take out the garbage, then you call my cousin Morty and ask for a job at the department store.

DR. DOOM: Then I can work on my Atom Destabilizer.

MRS. DOOM: Fine.

DR. DOOM: Thank you. And let it be known that the world will cower before Doom!

MRS. DOOM: Yeah, yeah. How about the garbage cowers before Doom?

(She pushes him off.)

NARRATOR 2: I fear marriage.

NARRATOR 1: You're probably not going to have to worry about it.

NARRATOR 2: Thank goodness. Wait, what?

PART 8: THE FANTASTIC FOUR

NARRATOR 2: Moving on. To the oldest superhero team of all time! Kind of. Maybe. We didn't do a lot of research. Not all of this should be taken as factually accurate.

BOY 2: Is it cool if I take notes on my phone?

NARRATOR 2: No.

GIRL: Is it cool if I take notes on my phone?

NARRATOR 2: Yes.

BOY 2: Hey!

NARRATOR 2: Double standard. Get used to it. Where was I?

NARRATOR 1: The oldest superhero team of all time. The Octogenarians!

(NURSE wheels in SCOTT, in a wheelchair, wearing his Cyclops red shades.)

NURSE: Okay Mr. Summers—we're going to have bingo tonight.

SCOTT: I don't want bingo. Where's the ice cream?

NURSE: We're not having ice cream tonight, Mr. Summers.

SCOTT: I'm 87 years old I can have ice cream when I want.

NURSE: It makes you gassy and that's not pleasant for anyone else, I can tell you that much.

SCOTT: You know what else isn't pleasant? When my glasses slip off my face.

(He slips his glasses down just as NURSE 2 enters.)

NARRATOR 1: Bzzzap!

NURSE 2: Aaaaaah!

(She falls down.)

NARRATOR 1: She's dead.

NURSE: Mr. Summers stop doing that!

SCOTT: What are you gonna do, put me in jail? I want ice cream, dang it!

NURSE: Fine. I'll get some.

SCOTT: And make it snappy, I don't have long.

GIRL: Is this an actual thing?

NARRATOR 1: Ha ha ha. Fine. No, the longest running superhero team is of course — The Fantastic Four.

BOY 2: Oh that was that bad movie.

GIRL: Yeah. I didn't see that.

BOY 2: It wasn't good.

NARRATOR 2: Don't judge them by their crappy movie adaptations.

NARRATOR 1: And they are: Mr. Fantastic!

(REED enters, waves.)

NARRATOR 2: Invisible Girl! Or Woman.

(SUE enters, waves, stands next to Reed.)

NARRATOR 1: The Human Torch, who can be black if he feels like it!

(JOHNNY enters, waves.)

NARRATOR 2: And the Thing, who we don't have a cool costume for so we're going to use this hand puppet!

(JILL enters, holding a Thing puppet.)

JILL: It's Clobberin' Time!

NARRATOR 2: We're not actually saying lines here yet.

NARRATOR 1: The Fantastic Four began in 1966, when four scientists —

JILL: I'm a scientist from Delancey Street and I'm stupid for some reason!

NARRATOR 1: Anyway, they went on a spaceship —

(Reed produces a toy spaceship and they all stand next to him.)

REED: There's radiation coming at the ship! Oh no!

SUE: Didn't you prepare for this?

REED: Um... I left our shield at home!

JILL: I'm gonna smash some heads!

REED: Well our enemy appears to be Cosmic Rays, Ben!

JILL: I'm smashing 'em anyway cause I don't understand stuff!

JOHNNY: I don't wanna die! Aaaaaaaaah!

ALL FOUR: Aaaaaaaaah!

NARRATOR 2: And, like all people who get hit with radiation, they developed super-powers that *The Incredibles* totally copied years later.

(Reed tosses the spaceship offstage.)

REED: I can stretch just like Elastigirl!

SUE: And I can turn invisible just like Shrinking Violet!

JOHNNY: And I'm hot! Hot damn! Call the po-lice and the fireman! Too hot!

NARRATOR 2: Shut up.

JILL: Agg! I'm even more disgusting now! No one's gonna love me!

REED: Ben, to be fair, no one was gonna love you anyway.

JILL: I'm callin' myself the Thing!

REED: Go for it.

NARRATOR 1: And they began adventures that have lasted for 50* years.

*(*Feel free to adjust this number.)*

NARRATOR 2: Now, they had many exciting adventures—crazy, psychedelic adventures that made no sense at all.

NARRATOR 1: In such made-up places as the negative zone, the microverse, the gamma zone, the betaverse, Earth 616, Earth 2105, an imaginary future, an imaginary past, and pretty much anyone their cracked out team of writers could come up with.

(WRITER 1 and 2 enter.)

WRITER 1: All right, so in this episode of the Fantastic Four they all turn into bananas.

WRITER 2: Whatever. I don't care. No one's reading this anymore.

WRITER 1: Done.

NARRATOR 2: And, like any show that's been going on for 50 years, the storyline got a little...

WRITER 2: All right, Sue and Reed's son grows up to be the most powerful human being on earth, and he travels back in time to when he was a baby to pretend to be the baby's nanny in order to make sure that he doesn't turn to the darkside, because in an alternate timeline he goes 3000 years into the future, enslaves humanity, and gets a big dog.

WRITER 1: Is this before or after they turn into bananas?

WRITER 2: Who cares?

WRITER 1: Cool.

(They leave.)

NARRATOR 1: It started to resemble a soap opera.

NARRATOR 2: So we give you... The Days of Our Fantastic Four.

(Soap opera theme music plays.)

NARRATOR 1: Like Sands in the Hourglass, these are the days of our Fantastic Four.

(Reed and Sue enter. They are very dramatic.)

REED: What is it, Sue? You seem...distant lately.

SUE: I have to tell you something. I don't want to hide anymore.

REED: Tell me. I can accept it.

SUE: You'll hate me!

REED: Probably.

SUE: Oh no!

REED: Please!

SUE: I'm not the woman you think I am.

REED: Are you a clone?

SUE: No.

REED: Secret double?

SUE: I got over that.

REED: Life-model decoy? Alternate version from the future? Time traveler pretending to be Sue? My daughter from a different line?

SUE: No no no and ewww!

REED: What is it then?

SUE: I'm having an affair.

REED: No!

SUE: With...

 (*Dr. Doom enters.*)

Victor.

DR. DOOM: Hello Reed.

REED: Victor Von Doom?! Nooooooo! Sue, he's a villain! Don't you see?!

SUE: He's changed his ways.

DR. DOOM: I'm good now. Promise.

REED: His last name is Doom. Doesn't that give you a clue?!

SUE: Victor is kind to me!

DR. DOOM: Would you like a kitten?

SUE: Ooh, thanks.

 (*He hands her a kitten.*)

REED: He's controlling your brain!

 (*Mrs. Doom enters.*)

MRS. DOOM: What's going on here?!

DR. DOOM: This is awkward.

SUE: No more lies! Victor and I are running off together!

 (*Johnny runs in.*)

JOHNNY: Wait a minute! I have something to tell you!

SUE: You can't change my mind, Johnny!

JOHNNY: You're my sister!

SUE: What?!

JOHNNY: I know!

SUE: That's crazy!

JOHNNY: Also! I might be black! Not sure, but it's possible.*

*(*This line may be cut.)*

REED: Dude, this was covered in our origin story.

MRS. DOOM: I have something to say too!

DR. DOOM: Honey.

MRS. DOOM: I'm not really your wife!

DR. DOOM: Who are you then?

MRS. DOOM: I'm really...the Silver Surfer!

DR. DOOM: No!

SUE: What?

JOHNNY: Who?

(Jill runs in with Thing puppet.)

JILL: It's Clobberin' Time. Probably.

MRS. DOOM: I'm afraid, Victor, that your real wife is imprisoned in an alternate dimension and I took her form in order to research life on Earth. I'm really Norrin Radd.

DR. DOOM: Norrin?

MRS. DOOM: Yeah, I'm a dude. My girlfriend was captured by my boss, Galactus. And he's keeping her hostage unless I serve him.

DR. DOOM: So wait a minute? Um...you're a dude under there?

MRS. DOOM: Freaky, isn't it?

DR. DOOM: Good thing I'm running off with this lady.

SUE: I have something to confess as well. I am also the Silver Surfer! From an alternate timeline! Sent here to stop this version of myself from bringing Galactus here.

JOHNNY: Who's Galactus?

NARRATOR 1: And at that moment, Galactus entered.

NARRATOR 2: He's like a thousand feet tall, by the way.

(An actor enters, holding an action figure of Galactus. It can really be anything.)

GALACTUS: I AM GALACTUS.

(Everyone looks up in the sky.)

(GALACTUS starts making little laser sounds.)

Pew! Pew! Pew!

REED: He's so huge!

JILL: This ain't my day.

JOHNNY: All right. Time to fight. Flame on!

REED: What does he want with us?

MRS. DOOM: He eats planets.

REED: Oh that's nice. What?

MRS. DOOM: Not like a teeth thing, you know. But like—he sucks the energy out of them.

REED: Oh. Well that makes a lot more sense.

DR. DOOM: Galactus! Hear me! I am Doom!

MRS. DOOM: He's not gonna listen to you.

(Galactus turns to slowly acknowledge Dr. Doom.)

Oh I guess I was wrong.

GALACTUS: SPEAK, HUMAN. Pew. Pew. Pew.

DR. DOOM: Um...don't eat Earth!

JOHNNY: Oh my gosh, Dr. Doom has turned into a hero!

JILL: I'm so confused!

GALACTUS: NAH, I'M STILL GONNA EAT EARTH, LOSER. Pew. Pew. Pew.

REED: There's only one way to stop him! We all attack at once! Combine our powers!

NARRATOR 1: And so they all combined powers and attacked.

(Everyone charges the action figure.)

GALACTUS: MEH. Pew. Pew. Pew.

NARRATOR 1: And Galactus defeated them all like he was swatting gnats.

(They all fall over at the same time.)

REED: It's no use! He's too powerful!

(Sue jumps in.)

SUE: Not so fast, my love!

REED: Sue?

SUE: Yes, I was just pretending to be an alternate timeline Silver Surfer, I'm really Sue Richards after all.

DR. DOOM: Oh thank goodness. I was really starting to question myself.

SUE: And I have been secretly having an affair with Galactus for the past five months.

REED: What?

GALACTUS: HEY BABY. Pew. Pew. Pew.

SUE: Sweetheart, I will be your new wife if you don't eat Earth!

GALACTUS: OKAY. Pew. Pew. Pew.

(Sue runs off with Galactus figurine.)

REED: Nooo!

JOHNNY: Sister!

DR. DOOM: Noooooo!

JILL: This makes so much sense!

DR. DOOM: I will now rededicate my life to evil.

MRS. DOOM: And finding your original wife.

DR. DOOM: Yeah whatever.

JILL: Wait. There's someone knocking at the door!

(A knock at the door.)

I'll get it.

(She moves off-stage for a moment.)

YOU?!! IT CAN'T BE!

REED: NOOOOOOOO!

NARRATOR 1: Who is it? We'll find out next episode!

NARRATOR 2: And they basically do that 600 times.

NARRATOR 1: Wow. No wonder their movies aren't very good.

PART 9: DOCTOR STRANGE

NARRATOR 2: Now at this point Marvel has learned that it can put anyone on the screen and people will go see the movie.

NARRATOR 1: Basically they're just punking us now.

(Two EXECUTIVES enter.)

EXECUTIVE 1: How stupid do I think the movie-going public is? Ant-Man.

EXECUTIVE 2: Nobody's gonna see that!

EXECUTIVE 1: Whatever, dude. We're Marvel. His powers are—he talks to ants.

EXECUTIVE 2: That's worse than talking to fish! No one's gonna see that!

AQUAMAN: HEY!

EXECUTIVE 1: And get this. He shrinks. And when he's shrunken, he has the strength of an ant.

(Executive 2 squishes an ant next to him.)

EXECUTIVE 2: Like this strong?

EXECUTIVE 1: Yeah, dude, some ants are like strong enough to lift a leaf.

EXECUTIVE 2: Aren't regular humans strong enough to lift a leaf?

EXECUTIVE 1: Fine, no Ant-Man. Okay get this: A talking duck.

EXECUTIVE 2: I'm listening.

EXECUTIVE 1: And he smokes and lives on a duck planet.

EXECUTIVE 2: How does a budget of a hundred and fifty million sound?

EXECUTIVE 1: Double it and you got a deal.

EXECUTIVE 2: Done.

NARRATOR 1: Which brings us to...

NARRATOR 2: Doctor Strange! Starring Overby Fumbletop. No I'm sorry that's Brindlesnug Mugglesnoot.

NARRATOR 1: Benedict Cumberbatch.

NARRATOR 2: Right.

(*DOCTOR STRANGE enters, wearing a cloak.*)

NARRATOR 1: There he is. Imagine him. Piercing blue eyes. Nose like an angel's knuckles. Fingers like an angel's nose. His accent soft and beautiful—as if his words were massaging you. Oh they're massaging you so much. Yess...

DOCTOR STRANGE: I respect you too much, [Narrator 1's name] to take advantage of you.

(*Narrator 1 makes a little squeaking noise of joy.*)

I have some poetry I'd like to read, if you don't mind the bother.

(*Narrator 1 makes another little squeak.*)

Might I move one delicate strand of your hair first?

(*He does.*)

NARRATOR 2: Anyway—

NARRATOR 1: Shut up shut your stupid face I'm imagining something.

DOCTOR STRANGE: Shall I tell you about my time playing Doctor Who?

NARRATOR 2: Doctor What?

DOCTOR STRANGE: Doctor Who.

NARRATOR 2: Who?

DOCTOR STRANGE: Yes.

NARRATOR 2: No, I was asking who.

DOCTOR STRANGE: Doctor Who.

NARRATOR 2: Who are you now?

DOCTOR STRANGE: Doctor Strange.

NARRATOR 2: Who?

DOCTOR STRANGE: No, Strange.

NARRATOR 2: Moving on! Doctor Strange is the Sorcerer Supreme of Earth.

NARRATOR 1: You are Supreme. Rarrr...

NARRATOR 2: How did he become Sorcerer Supreme, you ask? And what responsibilities does that entail?

NARRATOR 1: I don't care.

NARRATOR 2: Would you get back over here and continue the show? That's not even what's-his-face! That's an actor pretending to be Smugglenick Barbershop.

DOCTOR STRANGE: Shhh...

NARRATOR 1: Sorry. Call me.

DOCTOR STRANGE: I already have. In my heart. And my message is here.

(He points to his heart again.)

NARRATOR 2: So how did he become Sorcerer Supreme?

(ANNOUNCER enters.)

ANNOUNCER: And welcome back to the Earth Dimension's Got Talent! Today we are down to our grand finale — the three greatest magicians of the age! Let's meet them once again!

(DR. DRUID enters. He looks kind of like a portly professor-type. Bald.)

DR. DRUID: Greetings. I am Doctor Druid.

ANNOUNCER: Doctor Strange!

DOCTOR STRANGE: It's a pleasure to be here. I'd like to thank the elder gods who give me power—

ANNOUNCER: And the Scarlet Witch!

(SCARLET WITCH enters, chewing gum. She speaks with a Jersey accent.)

SCARLET WITCH: I would like to be known as Doctor Witch. Or Scarlet Doctor, whichever.

DOCTOR DRUID: You cannot just declare yourself a doctor, Witch.

SCARLET WITCH: I know for a fact this guy ain't no doctor.

DOCTOR STRANGE: I studied for centuries in a space outside of time with a Tibetan mystic.

SCARLET WITCH: Yeah, whatever.

DOCTOR DRUID: Silence, Witch.

SCARLET WITCH: How bout you shove it up your Druid-hole. Okay? I ain't above comin' over there and smacking the heck outta you. You know what a Druid is? It's a fruitcake that hangs out in the woods and kisses chipmunks.

DOCTOR DRUID: I do not kiss chipmunks. They are not cute. I have standards. Druids are deeply connected to the force of nature and we obtain our power—

SCARLET WITCH: Blah blah blah boring.

(She makes a motion with her hands.)

Hex!

DOCTOR DRUID: That didn't do anything.

SCARLET WITCH: It made you boring and stupid. Oh it worked!

DOCTOR DRUID: You have tangled with the wrong mystic, Witch. Behold my power!

SCARLET WITCH: Yeah last guy I dated said the same thing. Go back to the gym. You work out?

(She moves her hands again.)

Hex!

DOCTOR DRUID: Stop that!

SCARLET WITCH: Oh you don't like it, do ya? Hex! Hex! Double Hex!

DOCTOR DRUID: I have had enough of this nonsense! My Druid powers will see to your destruction!

SCARLET WITCH: Oh I'm scared.

DOCTOR STRANGE: I'm just standing here.

ANNOUNCER: People, please! Let's not see a repeat of the semifinal round.

(Enter MODRED THE MYSTIC.)

MODRED THE MYSTIC: Hey there! I'm Modred the Mystic and I will be sawing the entire audience in half.

(Terrible screaming sound.)

Oh. Um...whoops. Uh...hey are there are any janitors left?

(He runs off.)

ANNOUNCER: Again. Our thoughts go out to the families of the audience. We are very sorry for your loss. AND NOW! For the final determination, we shall see a demonstration of your magical powers! Spare no expense! Doctor Druid—you will go first.

DOCTOR DRUID: Very well. Allow me to warm up.

(He starts stretching.)

ANNOUNCER: We're actually live right now.

DOCTOR DRUID: Mee meee meee mee. The big black bug bit the big black bear—

ANNOUNCER: Live!

DOCTOR DRUID: Fine! For my final demonstration I will require... A VOLUNTEER!

(*CARLY sprints on. She may be located in the audience.*)

CARLY: Me! Meeee! MEEEEEE! YES! YES! WOO! WOOO! HELLO AMERICA! YES!

DOCTOR DRUID: Hello there—

CARLY: MY NAME IS CARLY AND I AM STOKED! WOOOO!

DOCTOR DRUID: Yes. Prepare yourself, Carly. The magic I am about to subject you to is—

CARLY: YESSSS!

DOCTOR DRUID: I haven't explained the magic yet.

CARLY: Sorry. Woo. Can I do a woo? I still want to do a woo.

DOCTOR DRUID: If you must, but —

CARLY: Woo!

DOCTOR DRUID: I will now exchange your consciousness with...an apple.

(*He produces an apple.*)

CARLY: Huh.

DOCTOR DRUID: You will feel no pain. Although this may render you permanently insane. I haven't done this before, so I'm not certain. But there are some chances it's important to take.

CARLY: So. Wait a second um —

DOCTOR DRUID: Zeeemargu Shambas Wobbo!

(Doctor Druid makes a weird series of gestures with his hands. Maybe the light flickers. Maybe there's a sound effect.)

(Carly stands there, motionless.)

(Doctor Druid holds the apple.)

DOCTOR DRUID: Carly, if you are in your own body, please wave.

(She does nothing.)

If you are in the apple, say nothing.

(He holds it up to his ear. The apple says nothing.)

The apple says nothing.

ANNOUNCER: Wow! So now what is — ?

DOCTOR DRUID: Silence. I am about to perform the second part of my spell.

(He holds the apple in front of him, focuses on it. He takes a big bite of it.)

(Carly falls down.)

ANNOUNCER: Ah!

DOCTOR DRUID: Oh come on. She was annoying.

(He takes another bite.)

ANNOUNCER: Stop what you're doing! Stop it!

DOCTOR DRUID: This is good.

(Carly leaps up.)

CARLY: I WAS JUST PRETENDING! WOOO! I NEVER WENT IN THE APPLE! Ha ha ha ha!

DOCTOR DRUID: Wait, no I —

CARLY: HELLO AMERICA! WOO! I'M GONNA CLAP FOR MYSELF!

(She runs off, clapping for herself.)

DOCTOR DRUID: Yes, well uh...that's...exactly how I wanted that to go.

(He exits.)

ANNOUNCER: Next up. The Scarlet Witch!

SCARLET WITCH: Doctor.

ANNOUNCER: The Scarlet Witch Doctor!

SCARLET WITCH: How about Doctor Scarlet Witch?

ANNOUNCER: Doctor Scarlet Witch!

SCARLET WITCH: Thanks. Uh yeah. I want to thank my Dad, Magneto, for this opportunity. He was really supportive of me even I though never saw him as a kid. Yeah. So what I'm gonna do for you now is tell you a story about when my magic was really awesome.

ANNOUNCER: I'm not sure storytelling is really what we're looking for —

SCARLET WITCH: Shut your pie hole before I use my magic to give you an ear there instead. Okay? Shut it.

ANNOUNCER: Shutting it.

SCARLET WITCH: Thank you. So all right — first of all — the guys around here are total losers, all right? So my friend Gina sets me up with her brother's friend, Tommy. Right? I don't know Tommy — I'm like, 'who's Tommy?' she's like, 'he's nice' I'm like 'he sounds like a loser.' Just cause of the name. I've never met a Tommy with a job.

So he shows up for our *(Air-quotes:)* date. I'm putting date in quotes right now cause what was about to transpire does not really qualify for the word. Okay, let me describe Tommy. First of all I can smell Tommy when he is a block away—this cloud of cologne comes down the street, comes to my house, opens my door by itself, and punches me in the face. Tommy is orange. He's got enough gel in his hair to suspend a horse from a bridge. He's got a tattoo over the top of his chest that says "The Greatest." How do I know what it says? Because he's wearing a tank top. For a date. I'm thinking nice restaurant, I'm wearing heels, I went tanning that day—to look nice, you know?

First thing he does, lifts up his shirt. Says, "feel my abs."

I'm like "no."

"Feel them."

"No."

"Feel them they're awesome."

"I'm not feeling your abs!"

"Wanda, I'm letting you touch me! Touch them, dang it! You know you want to!"

"No!"

"Fine. You know what? This coulda been the best night of your life. You just ruined it."

We go to the gym. Let me repeat that in case you didn't hear me properly: WE GO TO THE GYM. Starts working out. I'm making small talk, you know.

"You got a job?"

"I'm working on it."

"So that's a no."

"Why you gotta be judgmental? First date. You're judgmental! You want to judge something? Judge this." He takes his shirt off. Starts flexing and looking in the mirror.

First thing I do—a little hex—Start his tattoo on fire. Not like a lot of fire, you know? I'm not cruel—but enough—he freaks out, flames are popping out of his chest he's like "aaaaaaah! I'm burning! Help me!" Whatever. I'm like "stop, drop and roll"—he does that, cow falls on him. I don't have any control at this point. This 900-pound cow smashes through the ceiling, lands on him. Breaks a couple of his bones, whatever. He gets up, limping, still on fire, runs out into the street—aaaaaaah! Gets run over by a car. Another car hits him. This is Jersey, there's a lot of traffic. Here comes this semi next.

In the hospital later I set him on fire again. Just 'cause.

Later he tweets about it—like "that chick totally wanted me."

And that's when the airplane fell on him.

ANNOUNCER: Okay, thank you. I'm not sure what that has to do with magic, but —

SCARLET WITCH: You want to find out?

ANNOUNCER: Nope, I'm cool. And last up, Doctor Stephen Strange!

(Doctor Strange)

DOCTOR STRANGE: Thank you. Why do I deserve to be the Sorcerer Supreme, you ask? First of all, I hold the Eye of Agamotto, which grants me unlimited powers. And then there's the Rings of Raggadorr, the belt of Ishkun, and my favorite, the Girdle of Watoomb.

ANNOUNCER: What does that do?

DOCTOR STRANGE: It holds me. Tenderly. You see, when I entered the Negative Dimension to destroy the Faceless Ones and tackle the Dread Dormammu, I was forced to learn the secrets of the very weave of existence itself.

NARRATOR 1: You win!

NARRATOR 2: He hasn't even done anything!

NARRATOR 1: Let's just admit that the whole Doctor Strange thing is word salad, okay?

DOCTOR STRANGE: I also do card tricks. And...check it out.

(He produces a bouquet of flowers.)

Ta-da!

NARRATOR 1: Wow. I would like to discuss those spells with you backstage.

DOCTOR STRANGE: Of course.

(He escorts her off-stage.)

NARRATOR 1: *(As she's leaving:)* So do you have any tattoos?

ANNOUNCER: And I guess the winner is Doctor Strange!

PART 10: BATMAN VS. SUPERMAN

NARRATOR 2: All right then. Now one great thing that superheroes do is fight each other for no reason at all. Just for fun. X-Men versus Avengers. Avengers vs. other Avengers. Mutants vs. Hulk. Wolverine vs. Pretty Much Everyone. And...probably most famous — Batman vs. Superman.

GIRL: I thought we were doing Marvel right now.

NARRATOR 2: I'm sorry?

GIRL: Weren't we doing Marvel? Isn't that different than Batman and Superman?

NARRATOR 1: *(Returning:)* You've been paying attention?

GIRL: I think so.

NARRATOR 2: Wow. Well...yes this is DC, not Marvel but um...who cares? We're doing it anyway! Batman vs. Superman!

NARRATOR 1: It goes a little something like this.

(Batman and Robin jog in from one side of the stage.)

ROBIN: Caped Crusader, how can we possibly defeat Superman?

BATMAN: Do not fear, Boy Wonder. We shall use our minds, which are in just as tip-top shape as our muscular calves.

(Clark enters, opposite.)

You see, through the use of logic, I have deduced the secret identity of Man of Steel. It is none other than...

CLARK: Eye lasers. Blast.

ROBIN: Aaaaah!

(Robin dies.)

BATMAN: What have you done?

CLARK: Eye lasers again. Blast.

BATMAN: Aaaaaah.

(Batman dies.)

NARRATOR 2: Whoah. That was quick.

NARRATOR 1: All right, all right fine. Let's try it again.

(Batman and Robin run in.)

ROBIN: Caped Crusader, how can we possibly defeat Superman?

BATMAN: Well you see Boy Wonder—

CLARK: And I throw a pebble at supersonic speed, shooting it through your face like a bullet.

BATMAN: Aaaaah.

(Batman dies.)

NARRATOR 1: Take three!

BATMAN: Luckily, I have constructed a robotic exo-skeleton that is immune to Superman's eye lasers.

ROBIN: Holy Exo-Skeletons, Batman!

CLARK: Super breath knocks you over. I pick up the Empire State Building and I slam it on your face. You're dead.

(Batman and Robin die again.)

NARRATOR 1: Take four.

BATMAN: I have procured the substance which renders Superman mortal—Kryptonite.

ROBIN: Holy Deus Ex Machina, Batman!

CLARK: Laser vision melts the ground underneath you. When you sink into it I freeze it with my super breath. I pick up the Empire State Building—

BATMAN: Luckily I can—

CLARK: I move faster than the neurons in your brain. You can't react to me. Empire State Building on your head. You're dead.

BATMAN: Dang it.

NARRATOR 1: Take five!

BATMAN: Exo-skeleton, kryptonite, automated defense systems, portable force shield, super elastic tights.

CLARK: X-ray vision finds the weak spots. Laser vision carves you open like a can of sardines. Super breath blows your kryptonite away. I fly over and pull your elastic tights up in an atomic wedgie so devastating it splits you in half.

(Batman dies.)

ROBIN: Holy sh...

CLARK: And you're dead too.

NARRATOR 1: Take six.

BATMAN: Time out! Time out! Whoah. Time out!

CLARK: What?

BATMAN: Why are we fighting?

CLARK: I don't know. This whole thing makes no sense. I killed your girlfriend or something.

BATMAN: Oh that's right—

CLARK: Eye lasers. Super breath. Super speed. Atomic wedgie. You're dead.

BATMAN: Wait! Time out. You don't even know I'm about to attack!

CLARK: My super-hearing can hear the blood pumping faster in your veins as you prepare to take action. I can move faster than you can think, unleash my unstoppable powers, and kill you before you can do anything.

ROBIN: He's got us by the proverbial bird's nest, Batman.

BATMAN: I'm afraid I don't know what your homespun saying means, chum.

ROBIN: You know what I mean.

BATMAN: Ohhhh. Yes. Yes he does.

CLARK: Anyway, you're dead.

(Batman dies again.)

BOY 2: So basically Superman vs. Batman—

NARRATOR 1: Should've been like eight seconds long.

NARRATOR 2: Except we're all forgetting one crucial aspect of the 1960s style Batman: His utility belt.

NARRATOR 1: Oh... Take Seven!

(Batman and Robin run in.)

ROBIN: How are going to defeat Superman, Caped Crusader?

BATMAN: Fear not, Boy Wonder. Our utility belts contain the proper tools for just such a terrible battle.

CLARK: Eye laser.

BATMAN: Luckily, I have activated my Bat-Forceshield.

CLARK: Super breath knocks you down.

ROBIN: Not if our Bat-Anchors have anything to say about it!

BATMAN: Good one, chum.

CLARK: All right, fine, I move faster than speed of thought —

BATMAN: Not with our Bat-Mental-Accelerators, which we have already activated and I keep hanging on my utility belt here.

ROBIN: Those come in handy! Now I can pass Algebra!

BATMAN: Yes, Robin, it's important for you to continue your studies.

CLARK: All right I lift the Empire State Building and smash it on your heads —

BATMAN: Good thing my Bat-Empire-State-Building-Reducer was right here the whole time.

CLARK: What?

ROBIN: I was wondering when we'd use that.

BATMAN: Quick, while he's distracted, we can stop him if we both activate our Bat-Yellow-Sun-Blockers and Bat-Kryptonite-Laser-Nets!

CLARK: Aah!

BATMAN: Once again, we've learned a valuable lesson: Preparation is key.

ROBIN: And also—crime doesn't pay!

BATMAN: Oh Boy Wonder, you are a delight.

ROBIN: Thanks, Bruce.

BATMAN: Only call me that when we're alone.

ROBIN: Sorry.

BATMAN: Could you hand me the Bat-Kryptonite-Executioner's-Axe please?

ROBIN: Sure I can!

(Robin hands Batman an axe with a bat symbol on it—possibly the words "Bat-Kryptonite-Executioner's-Axe written on it.")

BATMAN: Shall I?

ROBIN: *(à la* Mortal Combat:*)* Finish Him.

(Batman brings the axe down on Clark's head.)

NARRATOR 1: The end.

NARRATOR 2: Wow.

NARRATOR 1: Just goes to show that an obsessed billionaire can basically bend reality to his will.

BATMAN: Let's go get the bat-donations-to-political candidates, Boy Wonder!

ROBIN: Woo hoo!

(They run off.)

PART 11: SPIDERMAN

NARRATOR 1: Well that pretty much does it.

NARRATOR 2: I hope you've learned something.

GIRL: I think so. But there were just so many superheroes!

NARRATOR 1: Seriously, that was like one percent of them.

BOY 2: What about Daredevil?

NARRATOR 2: He's just a blind dude.

BOY 2: Or *Ghost Rider*, starring Nicholas Cage?

NARRATOR 2: Let's all just pretend that didn't exist.

GIRL: I swear there's at least one more superhero we need to know about.

NARRATOR 2: Oh yeah. Right.

NARRATOR 1: Right. There's one more.

(Aquaman enters.)

AQUAMAN: Where do I come from, you wonder? Would you believe, the sea? Yes, I was a Prince of Atlantis once. Even though I'm a total white guy.

NARRATOR 2: Not you! Get off the stage, loser!

AQUAMAN: Just wait until you're near a stream, buddy! The goldfish never forget! Well, actually, yes they forget every three seconds or so, but there are other fish, and those fish are unfriendly!

(Aquaman leaves.)

NARRATOR 1: Now you may be familiar with this next character —

NARRATOR 2: Imagine a superhero that gets rebooted every three or four years —

NARRATOR 1: A story we're all familiar with, but they keep giving it to us anyway. Over and over and over again.

NARRATOR 2: Why? Because they think we're stupid.

NARRATOR 1: You know who we're talking about:

NARRATOR 2: Spiderman.

(SPIDERMAN enters. Maybe to the original theme song of his television show.)

SPIDERMAN: Just your friendly neighborhood web-crawler here.

NARRATOR 1: Spiderman has been the star of comic books, television shows, cartoons, 31 different movie versions—

NARRATOR 2: Seriously. They made a movie in the 70s—The costume doesn't even fit him, he's running around in this like red and blue jumpsuit. He fights homeless kids.

NARRATOR 1: And of course, a Broadway musical written by Boro and directed by Julie Taymor.

NARRATOR 2: Which was a disaster. Like, a hundred actors died during every performance.

NARRATOR 1: No they didn't.

NARRATOR 2: There were injuries. It was haunted. There was a lot of flying and stuff.

NARRATOR 1: So when you do a new version of Spiderman, you have to do something different.

NARRATOR 2: Yeah!

NARRATOR 1: You got an idea?

NARRATOR 2: Oh yeah. The problem with the musical...was that it wasn't big enough. Go big or go home. And when you think you've gone too big, go bigger than that. And when people are screaming at you to stop what you're doing for the love of all that is good, go bigger again.

NARRATOR 1: Can you even go bigger than the Spiderman musical?

NARRATOR 2: Oh yes you can. And when you want to go big, you go to the Germans.

NARRATOR 1: Like World War 2.

NARRATOR 2: No I was going to talk about the Ring Cycle.

NARRATOR 1: Never mind World War 2.

NARRATOR 2: It's 16 hours of pure musical annihilation. So, I give you: SPIDERMAN. THE GERMAN OPERA!!

(Narrator 1 whispers in Narrator 2's ear.)

I've been told that our budget cannot accommodate the truly mind-blowing things we want to show you. So! We're going to do a low-budget version—and when something is truly awesome, we're going to do our best to guide you through it. But we will have real elephants.

NARRATOR 1: We will not have real elephants.

NARRATOR 2: Will we have robot elephants?

NARRATOR 1: We will not have robot elephants.

NARRATOR 2: This is why Julie Taymor quit, by the way. Fine! I GIVE YOU: *(German accent:)* DIE SPIEDERMANN!

(Lights down.)

(What follows from this point, frankly, is insane. Imagine A Spiderman Opera created by Dieter, [Mike Myers' character from "Sprockets" on SNL] and you have an idea of the aesthetic at work here. Everything is overly dramatic, highly stylized, and barely comprehensible. Everyone, as much as possible, should

have a dramatic German accent. If you can't do a German accent, fake it.)

(Feel free to sing, opera-style as many of the lines as you wish. I have written singing in in only a few places to give you an idea. I have also suggested musical pieces at certain points, but you may use other music as well. Beethoven, Wagner, anything huge and bombastic will do.)

(The best versions of Die Spiedermann *[pronounced "Dee Schpeedermahn"] will use the script below as a starting point and find their own lines and movements.)*

(One last thing: Costumes. Feel free to experiment here as well. The black bodysuit with slicked-back hair, eyeliner, and lipstick that Mike Myers wore would be a great starting point.)

America. New York City. Now.

(OVERTURE: "Beethoven's 5th Symphony, 1st Movement.")

NARRATOR 1: Typical American High School.

(STUDENTS march in unison, singing to the Beethoven.)

STUDENTS: DIE SPIEDERMANN!
DIE SPIEDERMANN!
diespiedermann diespiedermann diespiedermann
diespiedermann diespiedermann diespiedermann
DIE SPIEDERMANN
DIE SPIEDERMANN
DIE SPIEDERMANN MANN MANN!

(They freeze and the music stops.)

NARRATOR 1: Behold: Peter Parker.

(PETER PARKER dances in.)

Gruesome outcast!

(The Students all suddenly point at him.)

STUDENTS: *(In unison:)* OUTCAST! HA! HA! HA!

PETER PARKER: It is too much!

NARRATOR 2: Behold Flash the Thompson!

(*Narrator 2 grabs Boy 2.*)

BOY 2: What? I'm not in the show!

NARRATOR 2: That's right! It is your worst nightmare! Audience participation German Opera!

BOY 2: Aaaahg!

NARRATOR 2: Flash the Thompson! Hero Man! *(To Boy 2:)* Say your line.

BOY 2: I don't know what my line is!

NARRATOR 2: LINE! SCHNELL!

BOY 2: Aaaaah! Parker. I thought we would meet here. In school.

PETER PARKER: Flash the Thompson!

FLASH THE THOMPSON: Yes.

NARRATOR 1: Enter Gwen Stacy!

(*Narrator 1 grabs Girl.*)

GIRL: What?

NARRATOR 2: Beauty made flesh.

GIRL: Thanks.

NARRATOR 1: Even though flesh must die. And Beauty is an illusion.

NARRATOR 2: She is blonde and hollow like a bird.

NARRATOR 1: Her scent is of baby flowers and despair.

PETER PARKER: I must love her.

NARRATOR 1: Say your line.

GIRL: I don't know what—

NARRATOR 1: SAY IT! LINE!

NARRATOR 2: *(Overlapping:)* SCHNELL!

NARRATOR 1: *(Overlapping:)* SCHNELL!

PETER PARKER: I must love her!

GIRL: *(Very quick:)* You cannot!

PETER PARKER: *(Very quick:)* I must!

GIRL: *(Very quick:)* You cannot!

PETER PARKER: *(Very quick:)* Nooooooo! *(Short pause.)* Why?

(*She runs to Boy 2.*)

BOY 2: Because she's mine!

GIRL: I do not wish to be possessed. And yet, the gazelle must yield to the lion.

(*MARY JANE WATSON enters.*)

NARRATOR 2: And who is this? Who comes? Who now is this? Behold: Mary Jane Watson.

MARY JANE WATSON: My hair is red like fire.

NARRATOR 1: She is cinnamon and chocolate.

NARRATOR 2: Her scent is of jasmine and confusion.

PETER PARKER: I must love you too.

MARY JANE WATSON: *(Very quick:)* You cannot!

PETER PARKER: *(Very quick:)* I must!

MARY JANE WATSON: *(Very quick:)* You cannot!

PETER PARKER: Nooo! *(Short pause.)* Why?

MARY JANE WATSON: Even the fire must be tamed.

(She runs to Boy 2.)

PETER PARKER: Oh come on. Seriously?

BOY 2: Come my ladies. We shall dance together like springtime in the summer.

(They dance off.)

ALL STUDENTS: OUTCAST. HA. HA. HA.

(They all exit.)

PETER PARKER: This cannot be! My life is over! Noooooo! But wait—Uncle Ben...Aunt May. Love. Home. Warmth. Yes. I will stay strong for you.

NARRATOR 1: Fate intervenes!

(Students, including Boy 2 and Girl, all enter in unison.)

STUDENTS: FIELD TRIP! FIELD TRIP!

(They sit, mimicking a bus.)

FIELD TRIP!

(A MAD SCIENTIST takes center stage.)

MAD SCIENTIST: Enter the radioactive zone if you dare! I shall permit no protective eyewear! Some call me mad. That is their right. I am the future, children. I will rule all time and space!

NARRATOR 2: We're getting a little too German here...

MAD SCIENTIST: I mean, um...look around. Please no photographs.

NARRATOR 1: And now...the descent of the radioactive spider!

(Everyone looks up and raises their hands.)

EVERYONE: *(Terrifying angelic noise:)* AAAAAAAH.

(*A GIANT SPIDER is lowered from the catwalks, or from a fishing pole of some kind.*)

NARRATOR 2: A hateful angel. A messiah of legs. It smells of Axe Body Spray and radiation.

PETER PARKER: Aaaaaha! Aaaaaaaaah! All is folly!

(*He wrestles with the Spider, running around the stage holding it onto his shoulder.*)

(*AUNT MAY and UNCLE BEN enter and grab him.*)

AUNT MAY: Peter!

UNCLE BEN: Peter!

PETER PARKER: Am I safe?

UNCLE BEN: There is no such thing as safe. There is only struggle and death. But yes you are home.

NARRATOR 1: And it was then—he made his fateful discovery.

(*Music.*)

(*He looks at his hands. Perhaps lifts something small.*)

PETER PARKER: I AM A LIVING GOD!

(*"Beethoven's 5ᵗʰ Symphony" again.*)

(*Everyone enters in unison and points at him.*)

EVERYONE: DIE SPIEDERMANN!
DIE SPIEDERMANN!
diespiedermann diespiedermann diespiedermann
diespiedermann diespiedermann diespiedermann
DIE SPIEDERMANN
DIE SPIEDERMANN
DIE SPIEDERMANN MANN MANN!

(Sudden silence. Everyone leaves in unison.)

NARRATOR 1: The bite of the spider's radiation gave him the strength of ten thousand spiders! The stickiness of a hundred spiders mashed into a paste! The danger detection ability of no spiders at all.

NARRATOR 2: He smells like hope.

(Peter Parker puts on some Axe Body Spray.)

And Axe Body Spray.

PETER PARKER: I AM SPIEDERMANN!

(Peter Parker runs out, jumps into the air -)

MARY JANE! GWEN! I SUMMON YOU! BECOME MY BRIDES!

(Mary Jane enters quickly.)

MARY JANE: No!

(She leaves, just as Girl comes in.)

GIRL: What am I supposed to say?

NARRATOR 1: No!

GIRL: No!

PETER PARKER: Dang it!

NARRATOR 1: There was no time for love!

NARRATOR 2: There is no such thing as love or time!

NARRATOR 1: But what dreams would our hero pursue?

NARRATOR 2: There are no heroes. There are no dreams.

(FAME [a person holding a large sign that says "FAME"] enters.)

FAME: I am Fame. I am a bitch.*

*(*Alternately, the line can be "I am Fame. I hate you.")*

(MONEY, a person holding a large sign that says "MONEY," enters.)

MONEY: I am Money. Worship Me. I am also a bitch.*

*(Or *I also hate you.)*

(LADIES, a man holding a large sign that says "LADIES," enters.)

LADIES: I am Ladies. I am pretty nice actually.

NARRATOR 1: Which would he choose?

(Peter goes to Money.)

NARRATOR 2: Not much of a choice really.

STUDENTS: DIE SPIEDERMANN!
DIE SPIEDERMANN!
diespiedermann diespiedermann diespiedermann
diespiedermann diespiedermann diespiedermann
DIE SPIEDERMANN
DIE SPIEDERMANN
DIE SPIEDERMANN MANN MANN!

(They exit quickly as the ANNOUNCER enters.)

NARRATOR 1: Scene change. A grimy gymnasium.

ANNOUNCER: Last five minutes with the Crusher! Two hundred dollars for whoever lasts five minutes with the Crusher! But really, what is time! How can only truly experience the passage of time! No one can! We are doomed to forget most of our lives! What was I saying!

(Peter strides in.)

PETER PARKER: I will take that bet.

ANNOUNCER: You will die!

PETER PARKER: No!

ANNOUNCER: Yes! BEHOLD: CRUSHER. He is the Man-Beast! He is Biblical in nature but cuddly at certain times! BUT NOW IS NOT ONE OF THOSE TIMES!

(CRUSHER enters. Crusher is a He-Man action figure held by someone skinny.)

NARRATOR 1: We wanted to build a robot here, but budget issues.

ANNOUNCER: BEGIN!

(DRAMATIC music.)

(Peter Parker stands opposite the action figure, which is motionless on the ground.)

PETER PARKER: Come on!

(The action figure does nothing. Peter Parker shouts at him.)

Who's afraid now? Of course I am still afraid of many things! Cancer! I'm totally afraid of cancer which is what one usually gets when bitten by something radioactive! So that's one thing I'm scared of! Also planes! And also, ironically, spiders!

NARRATOR 2: The Struggle. Of all life.

(Peter Parker grabs Crusher figurine.)

(He fights it, perhaps in slow motion.)

ANNOUNCER: Time is over. You are the champion. For now.

PETER PARKER: I AM A LIVING GOD!

ANNOUNCER: Perhaps. Perhaps not. Come on, Crusher.

(He picks up the action figurine and leaves.)

NARRATOR 1: Fate. For a second time.

(Dramatic music. ROBBER runs in, followed by two POLICE OFFICERS.)

POLICE OFFICER 1: That man is a criminal!

PETER PARKER: Aren't we all criminals in some sense?

POLICE OFFICER 2: Stop him!

PETER PARKER: Can one truly stop someone else? I do not know. I fear the questions so I do not answer them.

ROBBER: Hey thanks kid. You really helped me out.

NARRATOR 1: Those words.

(Robber slows into slow-motion.)

ROBBER: Thannnnks Kiddddd.

NARRATOR 2: They would haunt him. HAUNT HIM!

PETER PARKER: Noooooo! I AM HAUNTED!

(Uncle Ben enters.)

UNCLE BEN: I'll stop the robber!

ROBBER: Thannnnks Kidddddd.

(Robber shoots Uncle Ben.)

PETER PARKER: Nooooo!

(Uncle Ben falls to the ground as the Robber runs off. The Police leave.)

(Peter holds Uncle Ben.)

UNCLE BEN: Peter...is that you...?

PETER PARKER: This is the mask I present to the world.

UNCLE BEN: Does that mean it's you?

PETER PARKER: Yes.

UNCLE BEN: I am dying. If only someone had stopped that robber—if only someone had the strength to prevent this terrible crime—I bet that person would feel really, really guilty right now.

PETER PARKER: Maybe. I don't know.

UNCLE BEN: Because if they had acted I would still be alive.

PETER PARKER: Perhaps you would have been struck by a car moments later. Who can say?

UNCLE BEN: That person should still feel terribly guilty, though.

PETER PARKER: Maybe if you lived you would become a mass murderer, so the Robber did the world a favor by killing you.

UNCLE BEN: Peter. Promise me something.

PETER PARKER: It is folly to promise anything. I do not know my future self. I cannot bind him.

UNCLE BEN: Promise!

PETER PARKER: Fine!

UNCLE BEN: I want you to sew a red and blue costume for yourself, make it tight to show off your muscles but not too tight—cover your face in a mask, and I want you to swing around the city on ropes made of your own mucus.

PETER PARKER: Okay.

UNCLE BEN: And I want you to bring criminals to justice.

PETER PARKER: What if it's ambiguous whether or not they committed a crime?

UNCLE BEN: Okay in that case just punch them once.

PETER PARKER: Got it.

UNCLE BEN: I am dead. My last words will be…

(He dies.)

PETER PARKER: What?

NARRATOR 1: Irony! We never get to choose our last words. Our last words choose us.

PETER PARKER: Uncle Ben! I will do as you said! I will become a Superman.

NARRATOR 2: Stop saying that please.

PETER PARKER: I MUST BECOME DIE SPIEDERMANN!

(EVERYONE enters to the music again.)

EVERYONE: DIE SPIEDERMANN!
DIE SPIEDERMANN!
diespidermann diespiedermann diespiedermann
diespidermann diespiedermann diespiedermann
DIE SPIEDERMANN
DIE SPIEDERMANN
DIE SPIEDERMANN MANN MANN!

(They leave suddenly.)

PETER PARKER: First I must learn to sew! And then! The world!

NARRATOR 1: MONTAGE!

NARRATOR 2: MONTAGE!

(CRIMINALS run in as Peter Parker puts on a Spiderman mask.)

(THE DANCE OF THE HOODLUMS.)

(MUSIC: "Ride of the Valkyries.")

(It is best at this point if the Criminals are wearing tights, and/or stripey shirts, or other stereotypical criminal clothing.))

(They dance. The Criminals run about committing crimes, then turn on Spiderman.)

CRIMINALS: KILL THE SPIDER
KILL THE SPIDER
KILL THE SPIDER
AND DO SOME CRIME
KILL THE SPIDER
KILL THE SPIDER
KILL THE SPIDER
WE'RE CRIMINALS NOW

SPIDERMAN: I'M GOING TO STOP YOU
I'M GOING TO STOP YOU
I'M GOING TO STOP YOU
BECAUSE I CAN

CRIMINALS: NO YOU CAN'T

SPIDERMAN: YES I SURE CAN

CRIMINALS: NO YOU CAN'T

SPIDERMAN: YES I SURE CAN
I CAN SHOOT WEBS NOW
I CAN SHOOT WEBS NOW
I CAN SHOOT WEBS NOW
OUT OF MY HANDS

(Once the music gets to a slow point,)

NARRATOR 2: And inside his mind: The torments of his past!

ROBBER: Thannnnkssss Kidddddd...

UNCLE BEN: Myyyy last wordddsss are...

(Aunt May enters.)

AUNT MAY: Marisa Tomei is playing me in the next mooooovieee. Whattt the heckkkk?

BOY 2: I have twoooo girlfrieeeends...

AUNT MAY: Shee'ss like fortttty-niiiineee yearssss old.

GIRL: I don't knoooow myyyy lineeee...

STUDENTS: HA. HA. HA. HA.

(*The dance and music stops.*)

PETER PARKER: I keep fighting criminals. But I cannot fight...myself. Why have I been chosen to be the Superman?

NARRATOR 2: Spiedermann!

PETER PARKER: I would kill myself but my skin is so tough I would not succeed. At last I am a failure.

(*Girl runs in.*)

GIRL: Peter!

PETER PARKER: Am I Peter? Or am I the thing that prowls at night?

GIRL: Whichever.

PETER PARKER: Shouldn't you be with Flash the Thompson?

GIRL: I am cheating on him.

PETER PARKER: Cool.

GIRL: What am I supposed to say?

(*Narrator 1 whispers in her ear.*)

If love exists, and if I care to feel it, I would feel it with you. My being is a shell for my soul, and my soul screams in agony, and the only way to extinguish my nightmare is with your kiss.

PETER PARKER: I feel exactly the same way.

GIRL: What am I...?

NARRATOR 1: Kiss him. Audience participation requires that you kiss him.

GIRL: But—

NARRATOR 2: SCHNELL!

(Girl kisses Peter Parker.)

GIRL: Disappointing.

(She leaves.)

PETER PARKER: Wait!

(She stops.)

I was disappointed too!
Then again, all existence is disappointing.

GIRL: True. But you are particularly so.

(She leaves.)

PETER PARKER: I love you! If that exists.

(Mary Jane Watson enters opposite.)

MARY JANE: Peter!

PETER PARKER: I am hideous.

MARY JANE: That is what draws me to you. I am a mass of wicked tentacles. My heart is a meat grinder. My eyes are atomic bombs. Kiss me.

PETER PARKER: NEVER!

MARY JANE: YOU CANNOT RESIST!

PETER PARKER: I must!

MARY JANE: You cannot!

PETER PARKER: For all my power I am powerless!

(She kisses him.)

I must love you now.

MARY JANE: I must return to Flash the Thompson!

(She runs off.)

NARRATOR 1: By the way, no one does romantic comedy like the Germans.

NARRATOR 2: And now...The entrance of the Super-Villains!

(The SUPER-VILLAINS, the same people who played The Criminals, have donned very cheap-looking versions of the costumes.)

GREEN GOBLIN: I am Green Goblin. Do you fear me? Do you fear yourself? I am your id, the funhouse reflection of your own desire. Only one of us may live! Ha ha ha ha ha!

SANDMAN: I am the Man of Sand! Hold me? You cannot! Love me? You may. I am a metaphor for something, BUT YOU WILL NEVER KNOW WHAT IT IS. Ha ha ha ha!

BLACK CAT: I am the Cat Who is Black. I am a woman, and also a criminal. I also do not bear any resemblance to Catwoman, who is a villain in Batman. Ha ha ha ha!

ELECTRO: I am the Electric Man! That is all. I've got a lot of electricity.

DOCTOR OCTOPUS: I am the Doctor of Octopus! Ha ha ha. Oh, do you wish to know my secrets? Does an octopus have secrets? Perhaps you should ask him. Ha ha ha ha.

SUPER-VILLAINS: WE ARE THE VILLAINS. DID YOU CREATE US?

PETER PARKER: Noooo!

SUPER-VILLAINS: OR DID WE CREATE YOU?

(Other people from his past come forward.)

UNCLE BEN: Myyyy lassst worrrrds are...

MARY JANE: Myyy eyesss are atttomicc bommbbbss...

ROBBER: Thannnkss kidddd...

AUNT MAY: Marrissssa freakinnnngg Tommeeeeeiii...

(Aquaman enters.)

AQUAMAN: I cannn tallkkk to fisssssh...

NARRATOR 1: And now we begin...the final battle!

(Carmina Burana plays.)

SUPER-VILLAINS: WE'LL GET YOU NOW
WE'LL KICK YOUR BUTT
WE HAVE SO MANY SUPER-POWERS!

(Peter Parker runs around to confront them in a dancing-like fashion.)

(SUPER-VILLAINS begin a slow chant as Spiderman chases them. The GREEN GOBLIN grabs Girl.)

GREEN GOBLIN: I'll just randomly capture this random girl you probably don't care about!

PETER PARKER: Gwen! It is like a funhouse mirror where all my desires are reflected with monstrous clarity!

MARY JANE: What about me?

PETER PARKER: I like you too!

SUPERVILLAINS: *(Continuous chant:)* WE'LL GET YOU NOW
WE ARE SO COOL
WE WEAR TIGHT-FITTING CLOTHING
WE'VE GOT BIG PLANS
WE DON'T KNOW WHAT
WE DON'T DO MUCH ON WEEKENDS

AND WE'LL FIGHT YOU
IN DISCOTEQUES
EVEN THOUGH THAT IS A FRENCH PLACE
DO YOU SPEAK FRENCH?
I DON'T SPEAK FRENCH
THEN WHY'D WE MENTION THE DISCO?
NONE OF US MAKE SENSE
WE SHOULD LEAVE NEW YORK
AND TAKE OVER A DIFFERENT COUNTRY
LET'S ROB A BANK
INSTEAD OF FIGHT THIS JERK
HOW BOUT IDENTITY THEFT

GREEN GOBLIN: Stay back!

PETER PARKER: Release her! Kill me instead!

GREEN GOBLIN: Okay.

(He drops Girl.)

NARRATOR 1: She falls!

GIRL: Aaaah!

PETER PARKER: I must save her with my mucus! It is disgusting yet useful!

(He catches Girl with his web.)

NARRATOR 2: SNAP!

NARRATOR 1: OH SNAP!

NARRATOR 2: HER NECK!

NARRATOR 1: OH SNAP!

SPIDERMAN: Nooo!

(Spiderman sinks to his knees.)

GREEN GOBLIN: Now villains! While he is experiencing weltschmerz! Kill the Spider!

(Aquaman bursts in as the music crescendos again.)

AQUAMAN: I'M AQUAMAN!
YES AQUAMAN!
YOU THOUGHT I WAS A PANSY!
BUT CHECK THIS OUT!
I TALK TO FISH!
SO SUCK ON THIS SHARKNADO!

(The Sharknado attacks! Make this is as big as possible. If you have catwalks, perhaps the sharks fly down from the catwalks, perhaps they are thrown in from off-stage. Perhaps fish are thrown. Maybe there are flashpots and smoke. Go as big as possible.)

IT'S FLYING SHARKS
THEY REALLY BITE
THEY'RE GONNA EAT YOUR FACE OFF!
YES SHARKNADO!
SING SHARKNADO!
HERE THEEEEEEEY COME!

(The villains run around with sharks attached to them, screaming and dying. Again, maybe there's spurting blood at this point.)

(All of them die.)

(Music ends dramatically.)

AQUAMAN: That's what I'm talking about. Mic drop.

(He drops a fish. Walks off.)

(Peter Parker holds Girl, who is dead.)

PETER PARKER: Her neck. I broke her neck.

MARY JANE: I love you more for this. Your loss makes you irresistible.

PETER PARKER: Not now Mary Jane! I... Loved... Her...if love is an illusion then I loved the illusion of love. She is no more. Dead forever.

(The ghost of Uncle Ben enters.)

UNCLE BEN: I would like to point out the irony that your own powers killed her.

PETER PARKER: Noooo!

UNCLE BEN: Yessss! Ha ha ha ha.

(Aunt May enters.)

AUNT MAY: Peter?

PETER PARKER: Aunt May?

AUNT MAY: Let's go home. I am old, like Marisa Tomei, and I need to rest.

PETER PARKER: Okay, Aunt May.

(Boy 2 enters.)

BOY 2: Parker. What have you done?!

PETER PARKER: Leave me alone, Flash the Thompson!

BOY 2: Noo!

PETER PARKER: Yes!

BOY 2: Okay!

(Peter stays on his knees as Narrator 1 and 2 returns.)

NARRATOR 1: Well I hope you learned something.

NARRATOR 2: There is no such thing as knowledge.

GIRL: Um... I think so. I should be cool enough to date nerds now.

BOY 2: Me too! I think. Wait...

NARRATOR 1: But there's one last thing you need to know...

(Peter Parker stays on his knees.)

PETER PARKER: I will no longer be the happy-go-lucky Peter you once knew. Now, now I shall wear...

(Someone runs in with Spiderman's black suit.)

Black!

(Batman enters.)

BATMAN: Yeah, it happens.

(Batman picks up a rubber shark, looks at it.)

NARRATOR 2: Don't touch that shark, it's stuffed with explosives!

BATMAN: That's crazy.

(Batman punches it in the face.)

(BOOM!)

(Lights down. End of play.)

The Author Speaks

What inspired you to write this play?
I know it's shocking to contemplate, but I was quite a dork when I was younger. I was into basically everything that stereotypical nerds were into in varying degrees. It's amused me to no end to see everything that nerdy kids loved in the 80s and 90s slowly make its way into popular culture, and even to dominate it. So I wanted to make fun of the fact that superheroes are everywhere, and at the same time deal with some characters that I loved as a kid.

Was the structure or other elements of the play influenced by any other work?
Yes, this play is loosely similar to another play of mine, *The Brothers Grimm Spectaculathon*, which in turn was inspired by the *Complete Works of William Shakespeare (abridged)*. The cast has grown considerably, but I certainly look to the structure of those plays.

Have you dealt with the same theme in other works that you have written?
Oddly enough, I haven't written about superheroes before. I've done a lot of work with fairy tales and myths, which are similar to superheroes. Soap operas are also remarkably similar to comic books, because they've both got stories that have to keep going for years and years.

What writers have had the most profound effect on your style?
Christopher Durang and David Lindsay-Abaire stand out to me. And of course, Bobby Lopez and his twin masterpieces, *Avenue Q* and *The Book of Mormon*.

What do you hope to achieve with this work?
Global domination. I think I always say that actually. No – I'm really hoping to give people a large, really fun show. I want

people to have fun on stage and I want the audience to enjoy the experience.

What were the biggest challenges involved in the writing of this play?
Two things: costumes and parts for women. I make the joke over and over again that very few superheroes are female, and the ones that are often forced into wearing ridiculous outfits that no real-world human could fit into. So I consciously chose to add as many other roles for actresses as possible—I allow for the possibility, of course, that any male superhero in the show could be played by a woman, but I wanted the show to deal with the sexism inherent in the industry.

Now that comics are such huge business (well, comics aren't, but the movies derived from comic books are) I think it's really important to keep the sexism in check. I think of myself as a feminist playwright, and I love to challenge the Hollywood culture that casts men as 70% of all speaking roles. So I keep bringing that up.

The costumes are also going to be a challenge with the show. It's almost impossible to get them all to look right, but it might be really cool if you could. So I think that you either go very basic with the costumes, or, if you've got that kind of budget, go awesome with them. I think pretty good costumes is not the way to go with this one.

What are the most common mistakes that occur in productions of your work?
The biggest thing for me is watching actors who know they're funny on stage. I hate it when they mug for the audience, or give a little wink wink "aren't I funny?" For the most part, comedy is serious business. The characters are funny because they're serious, so you can't play it for the laughs. You have to play the deadly seriousness of it.

I think that's critically important in the insane German opera section of this show. That must be deadly serious, without a hint of a smile from anyone. If you laugh at it while you're performing it, it simply won't work.

What inspired you to become a playwright?
I started out as an actor and was interested in writing novels, actually. When I figured out that I could get an immediate reaction from an audience if I put it onstage (instead of waiting and pestering people for a response), I was hooked.

How did you research the subject?
Well, as I said earlier, I was a pretty huge dork, so I knew just about everything I needed to know about superheroes. Comics did some crazy things in the 2000s, but I basically ignored all of that and went back to the earlier age of comics – (1960s-1990s) – I feel like the movies we're watching today are based on that earlier version of the superheroes and not the most current version.

Are any characters modeled after real life or historical figures?
Benedict Cumberbatch I guess, since he will be playing Doctor Strange.

About the Author

Don Zolidis holds a B.A. in English from Carleton College and an M.F.A. in playwriting from the Actor's Studio Program at the New School University, where he studied under Romulus Linney. His plays have been seen at numerous theatres around the country, including The Purple Rose Theatre, The Ensemble Studio Theatre, The Phoenix Theatre, the Victory Theatre, Stage West, The Williamstown Theatre, and many others. Don received the Princess Grace Award for playwriting in 2004 after having twice been a finalist. His plays have received two Edgerton New Play awards and multiple NEA grants among other honors. In 2013 his play **White Buffalo** was nominated for the Pulitzer Prize for Drama. His plays for young people are among the most-produced in the country and have received more than 7,000 productions, appearing in every state and 51 countries.

About YouthPLAYS

YouthPLAYS (www.youthplays.com) is a publisher of award-winning professional dramatists and talented new discoveries, each with an original theatrical voice, and all dedicated to expanding the vocabulary of theatre for young actors and audiences. On our website you'll find one-act and full-length plays and musicals for teen and pre-teen (and even college) actors, as well as duets and monologues for competition. Many of our authors' works have been widely produced at high schools and middle schools, youth theatres and other TYA companies, both amateur and professional, as well as at elementary schools, camps, churches and other institutions serving young audiences and/or actors worldwide. Most are intended for performance by young people, while some are intended for adult actors performing for young audiences.

YouthPLAYS was co-founded by professional playwrights Jonathan Dorf and Ed Shockley. It began merely as an additional outlet to market their own works, which included a substantial body of award-winning published and unpublished plays and musicals. Those interested in their published plays were directed to the respective publishers' websites, and unpublished plays were made available in electronic form. But when they saw the desperate need for material for young actors and audiences—coupled with their experience that numerous quality plays for young people weren't finding a home—they made the decision to represent the work of other playwrights as well. Dozens and dozens of authors are now members of the YouthPLAYS family, with scripts available both electronically and in traditional acting editions. We continue to grow as we look for exciting and challenging plays and musicals for young actors and audiences.

About ProduceaPlay.com

Let's put up a play! Great idea! But producing a play takes time, energy and knowledge. While finding the necessary time and energy is up to you, ProduceaPlay.com is a website designed to assist you with that third element: knowledge.

Created by YouthPLAYS' co-founders, Jonathan Dorf and Ed Shockley, ProduceaPlay.com serves as a resource for producers at all levels as it addresses the many facets of production. As Dorf and Shockley speak from their years of experience (as playwrights, producers, directors and more), they are joined by a group of award-winning theatre professionals and experienced teachers from the world of academic theatre, all making their expertise available for free in the hope of helping this and future generations of producers, whether it's at the school or university level, or in community or professional theatres.

The site is organized into a series of major topics, each of which has its own page that delves into the subject in detail, offering suggestions and links for further information. For example, Publicity covers everything from Publicizing Auditions to How to Use Social Media to Posters to whether it's worth hiring a publicist. Casting details Where to Find the Actors, How to Evaluate a Resume, Callbacks and even Dealing with Problem Actors. You'll find guidance on your Production Timeline, The Theater Space, Picking a Play, Budget, Contracts, Rehearsing the Play, The Program, House Management, Backstage, and many other important subjects.

The site is constantly under construction, so visit often for the latest insights on play producing, and let it help make your play production dreams a reality.

More from YouthPLAYS

Les Examables by Don Zolidis

Comedy. 100-110 minutes. 8-28 females, 5-25 males (15-40+ performers possible).

Tired of too much standardized testing in her high school, high achiever Anna Ullman stages a protest and finds herself crowned the new principal. But ultimate power comes with its own problems (especially after death threats from the all-powerful State Board of Ed), and soon Anna descends into madness, imposing even more standardized testing. It's up to her former best friend, Lola, to bring down this new tyrant. Soon Lola is manning the barricades and singing triumphantly awesome songs in this insane satire based on the mega-musical *Les Misérables*.

The Exceptional Childhood Center by Dylan Schifrin

Comedy. 25-35 minutes. 2-4 females, 2-3 males (5-6 performers possible).

Reggie Watson has been accepted into the right preschool. He's set for life…as long as he can make it through the one-day trial period. But when desperation breeds disaster and his future hangs in the balance, Reggie and his band of quirky classmates may just discover things about themselves that school could never teach them.

Slow by Keegon Schuett

Drama. 45-55 minutes. 1 male, 3 females, 1 either.

Lizzy Slominski's classmates call her "Camera Girl," because she's always hiding behind her camera snapping photos of strangers. But when a mysterious new boy appears at the bus stop, will she be able to put down her camera and connect, or is she doomed to a life of observing through the lens?

The Locker Next 2 Mine by Jonathan Dorf
Dramedy. 80-85 minutes. 5-12+ males, 8-16+ females (14-40 performers possible).

Alisa arrives at a new high school in the middle of the year to find her locker next to a shrine for a popular lacrosse player who's died in an auto accident, but as she digs deeper, she discovers another death that no one talks about, even as it's left many of the school's students trying to pick up their own pieces. A play about teen suicide and dealing with loss.

The Matsuyama Mirror by Velina Hasu Houston
Drama. 60-70 minutes. 4 females, 1 male, 3 either.

In Matsuyama, Japan in the 1600s, a world before the discovery of mirrors, young Aiko comes of age in the aftermath of her mother's death. Gifted with a "magic" mirror, she sees her image and believes that it is her mother's spirit—and when her father remarries and she begins to grow up, Aiko resists, escaping into an enchanted world where dolls come to life. As they encourage her to stay to play and frolic, will Aiko fall into the fantasy forever, or will she discover the true magic of life?

What Happened at the Mud Puddle by Tara Meddaugh
Comedy. 25-30 minutes. 8 females, 4 males.

Taylor and Chloe are lifelong friends. Or they were—until Taylor throws an over-the-top yacht party the same day as Chloe's birthday party. Despite Taylor's rep, no one wants to turn down an extravagant candy station, a concert from the hottest band or pricey swag. But before the boat even leaves the dock, Taylor turns on her guests as only a mean girl can. It's shiny toys vs. backyard ice cream as friendships are tested, and of course, someone meets a mud puddle.

ShakeSPLOSION!!! by Andrew Geha

Comedy. 75-85 minutes. 9-21+ females, 4-14+ males (14-100+ performers possible).

ShakeSPLOSION!!! is a madcap sprint through every play written by the Bard. From 235 years of English kings in the History Plays, to (nearly) every bloody death in the Tragedies, to every girl who dressed up as a boy in the Comedies, it's like watching Shakespeare's entire canon fired out of a cannon—scattering prose, verse and characters across the stage. Sword fights! Word fights! Witches, ghosts and murder! All in 80 minutes!! Performed by teenagers!!!

Of Plastic Things and Butterfly Wings by Greg Romero

Young Audiences. 45-50 minutes. 2-10 males, 3-10 females (2-20 performers possible).

A plastic water bottle named Sam has lost her parents in The Gyres, a swirling ocean landfill twice the size of Texas. With help from a blue crab with a giant claw, a parrot who thinks she is a seagull, and The Oldest Sea Turtle That Ever Lived, Sam embarks on a family-friendly, music-filled, epic journey to save us all from the lonely, swirling vortex of thrown-away things and lost hope.

Girls on the Brink by Rex McGregor

Dramedy. 70-80 minutes. 4-23 females, 0-8 males (4-23 performers possible).

A collection of short plays about coming of age and the dramatic impact of sudden change on young lives. From a new take on **Romeo and Juliet** to an Afghan girl whose days as a boy are at an end to a futuristic tale of living forever, these seven very different plays all explore that precarious moment when young people find themselves on the brink of life

Made in the USA
San Bernardino, CA
18 March 2020

65625011R00066